GIANT CATS & BIG DOGS

COLORING BOOK FOR ADULTS

Cats Coloring Book For Adults

GIANT CATS

Fantasy Art Coloring Book For Stress Relief

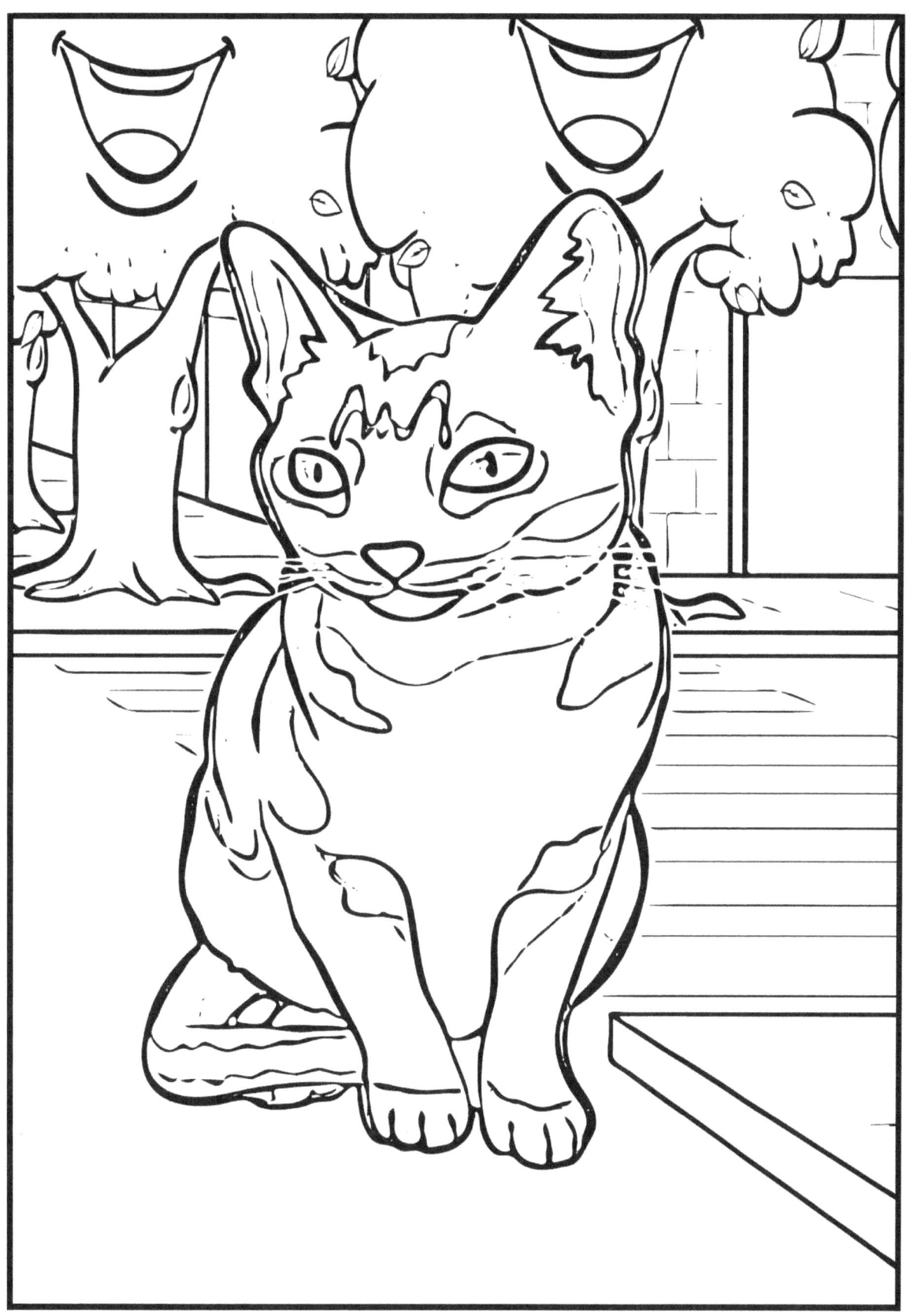

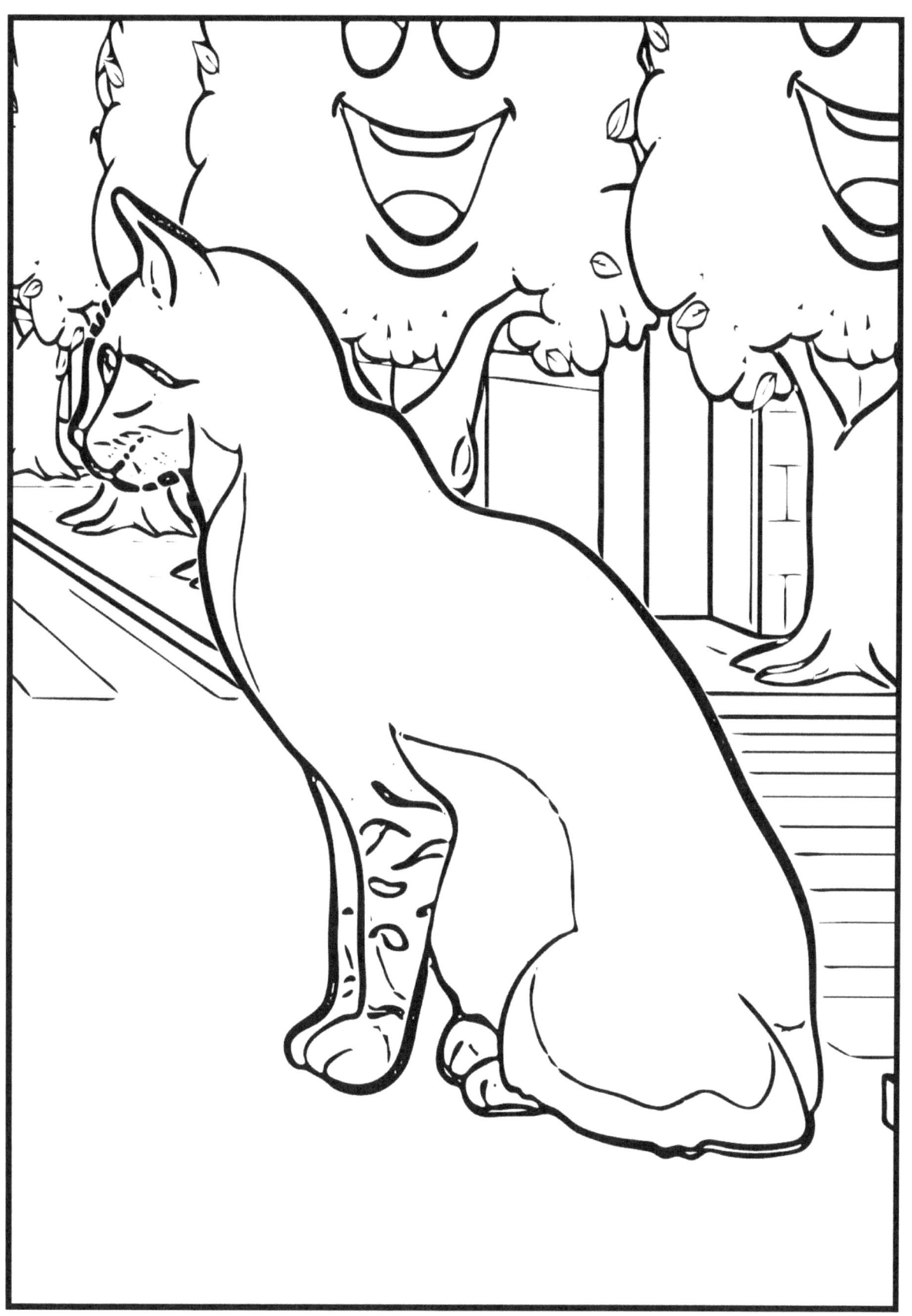

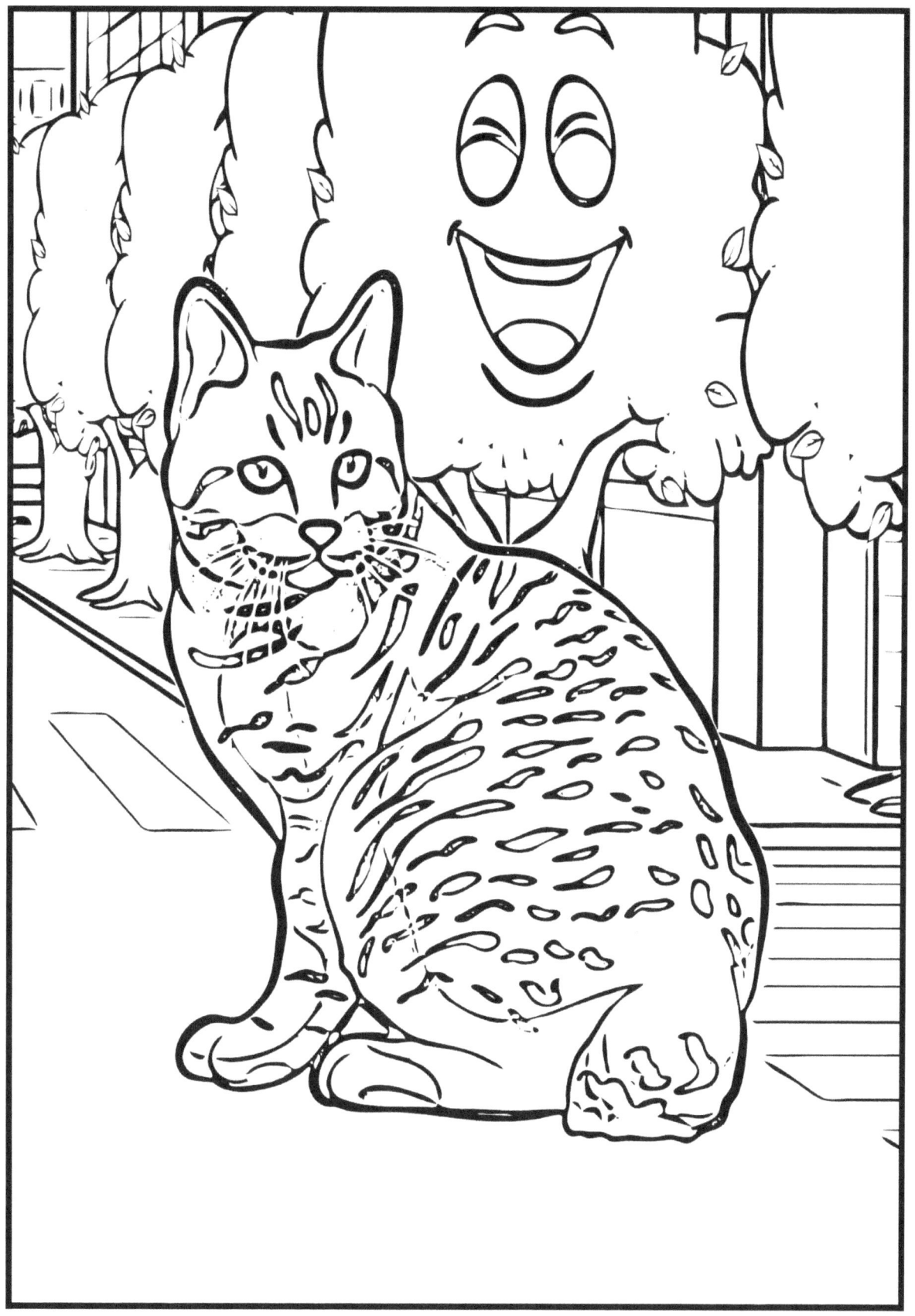

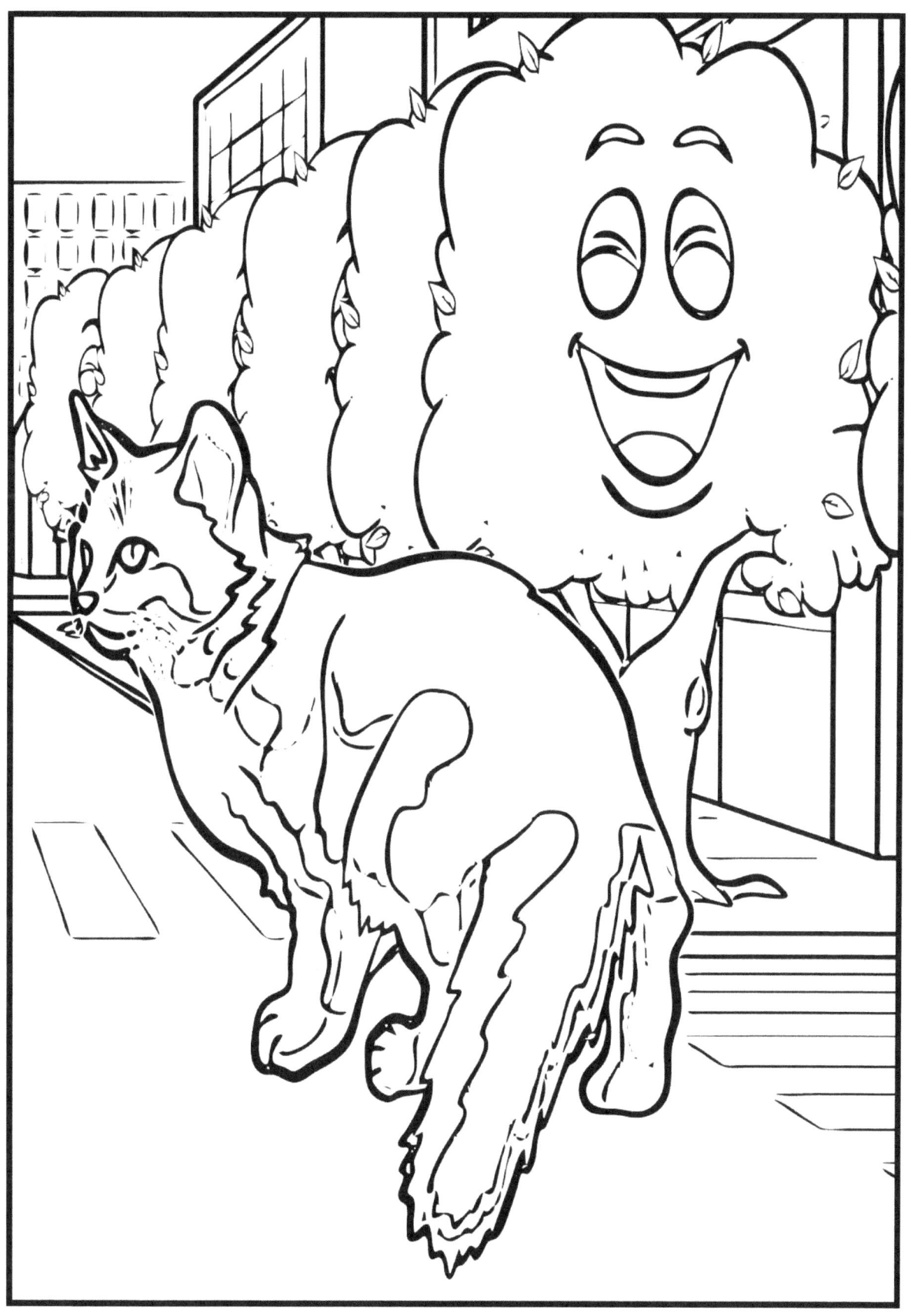

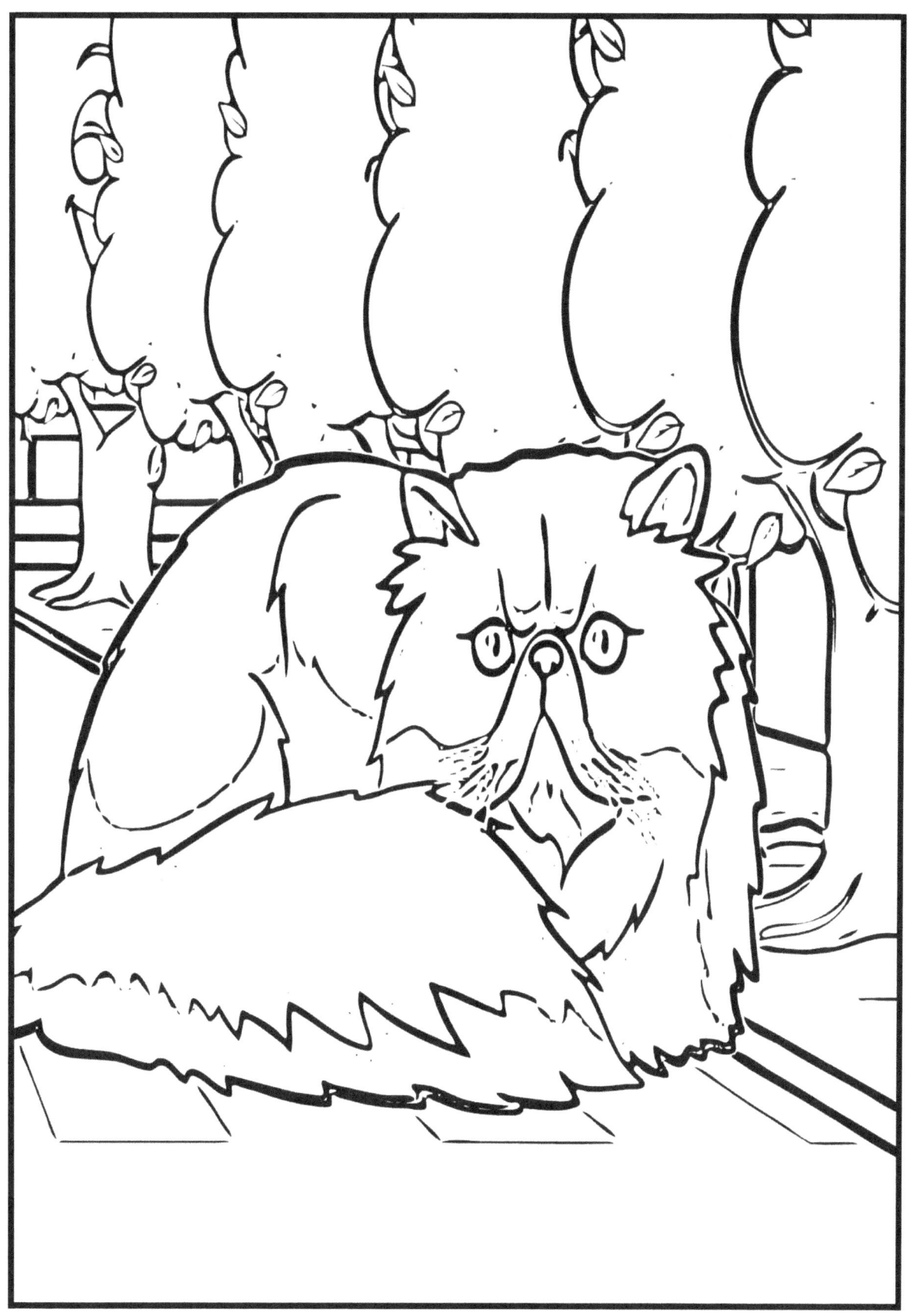

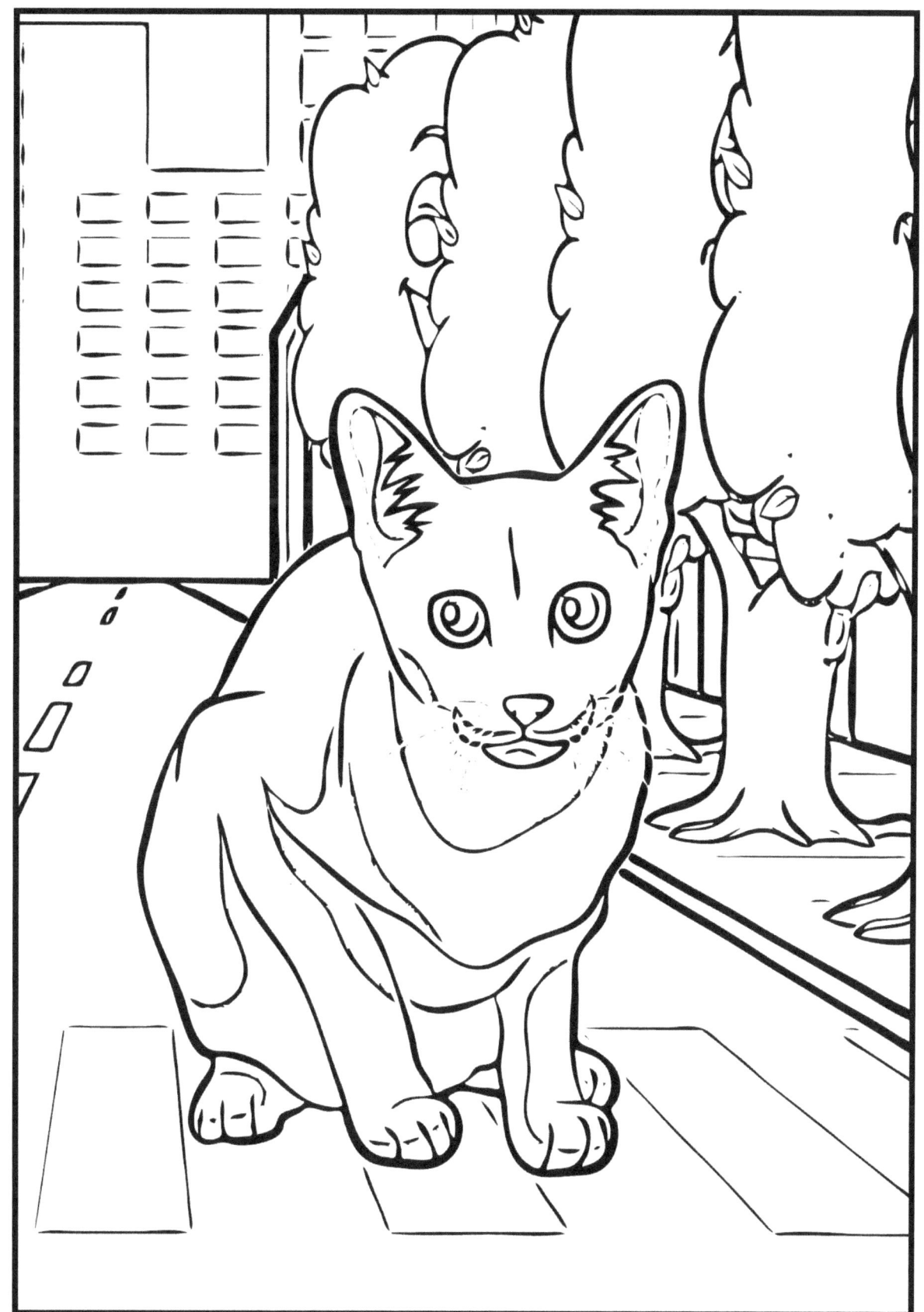

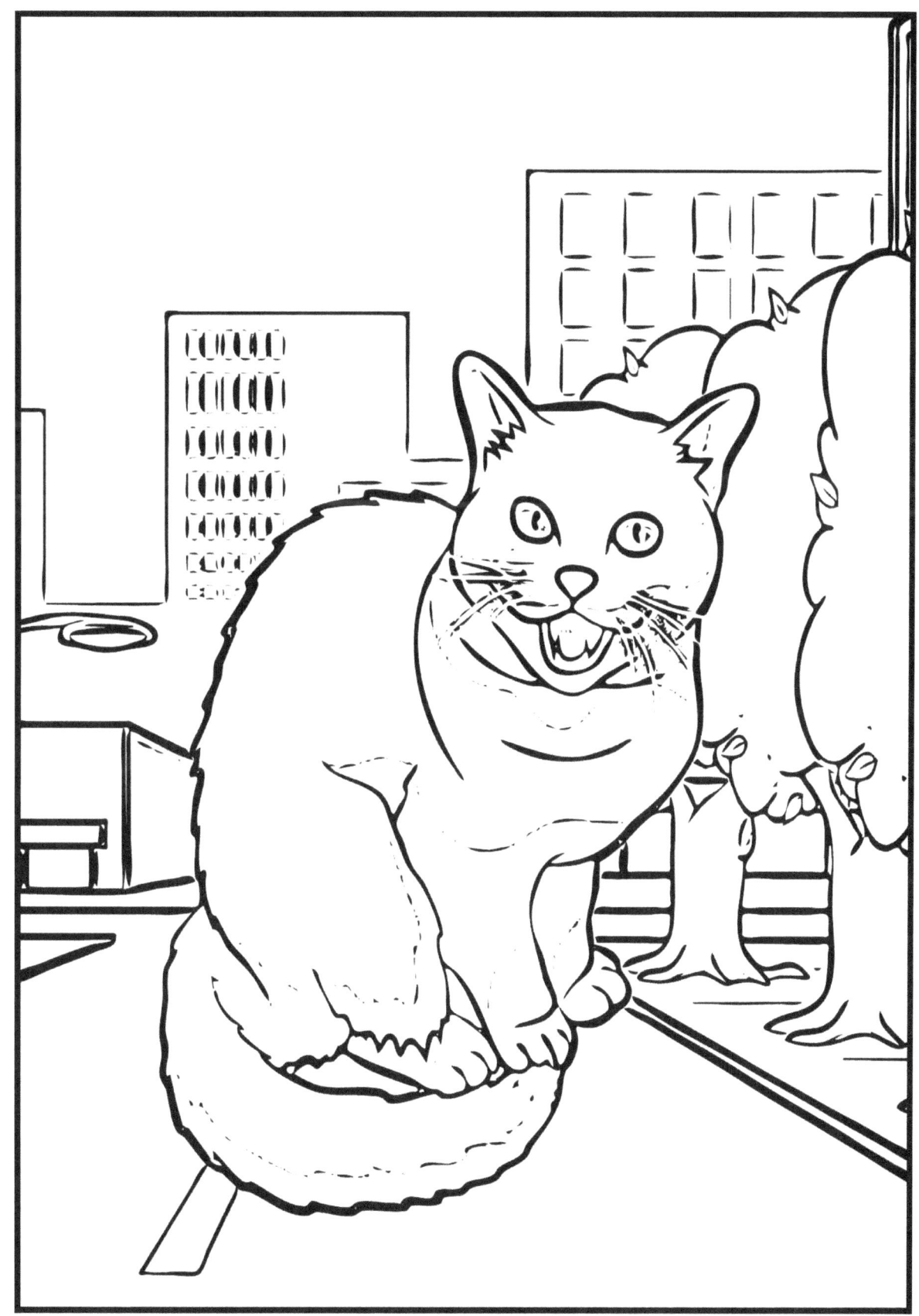

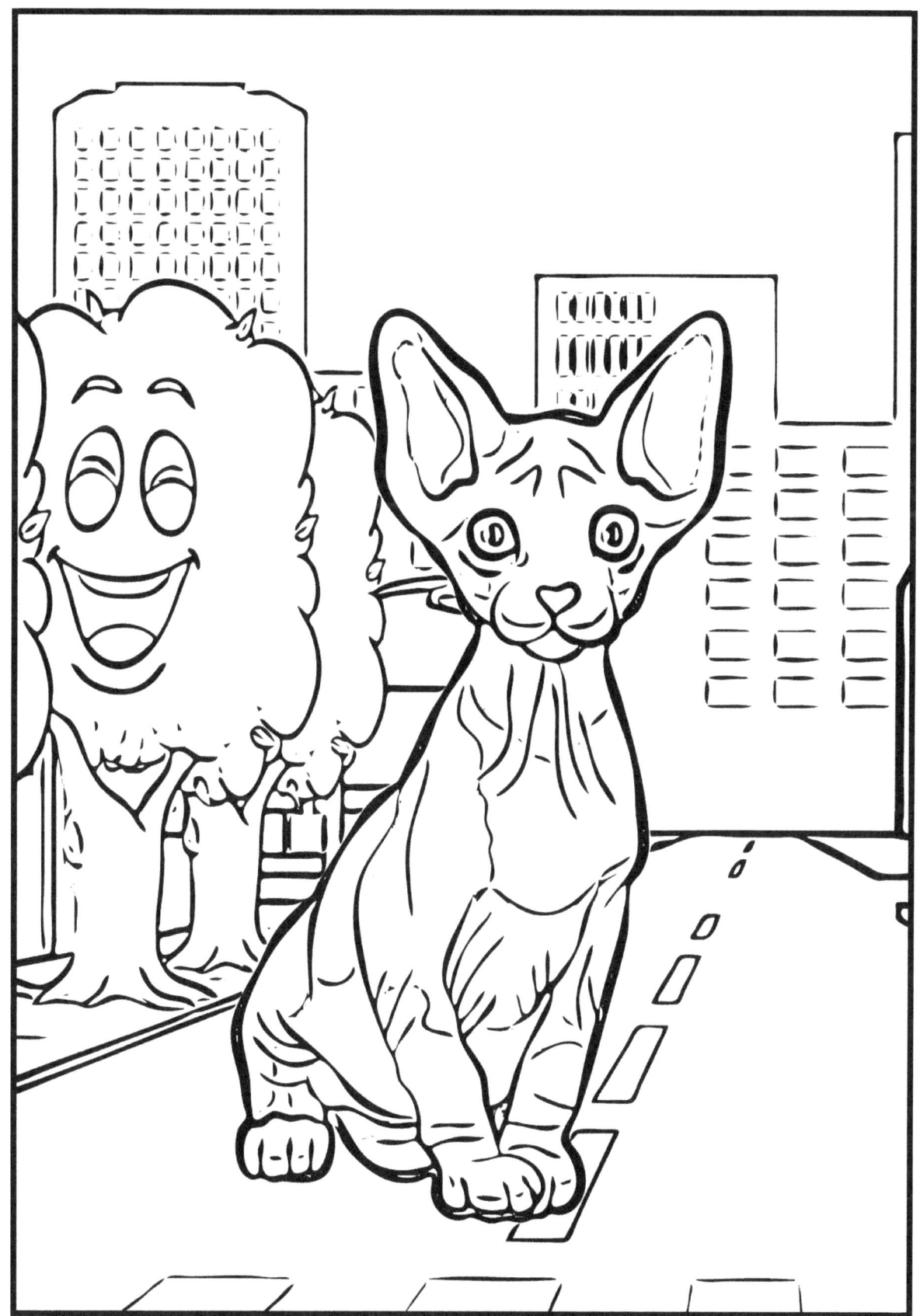

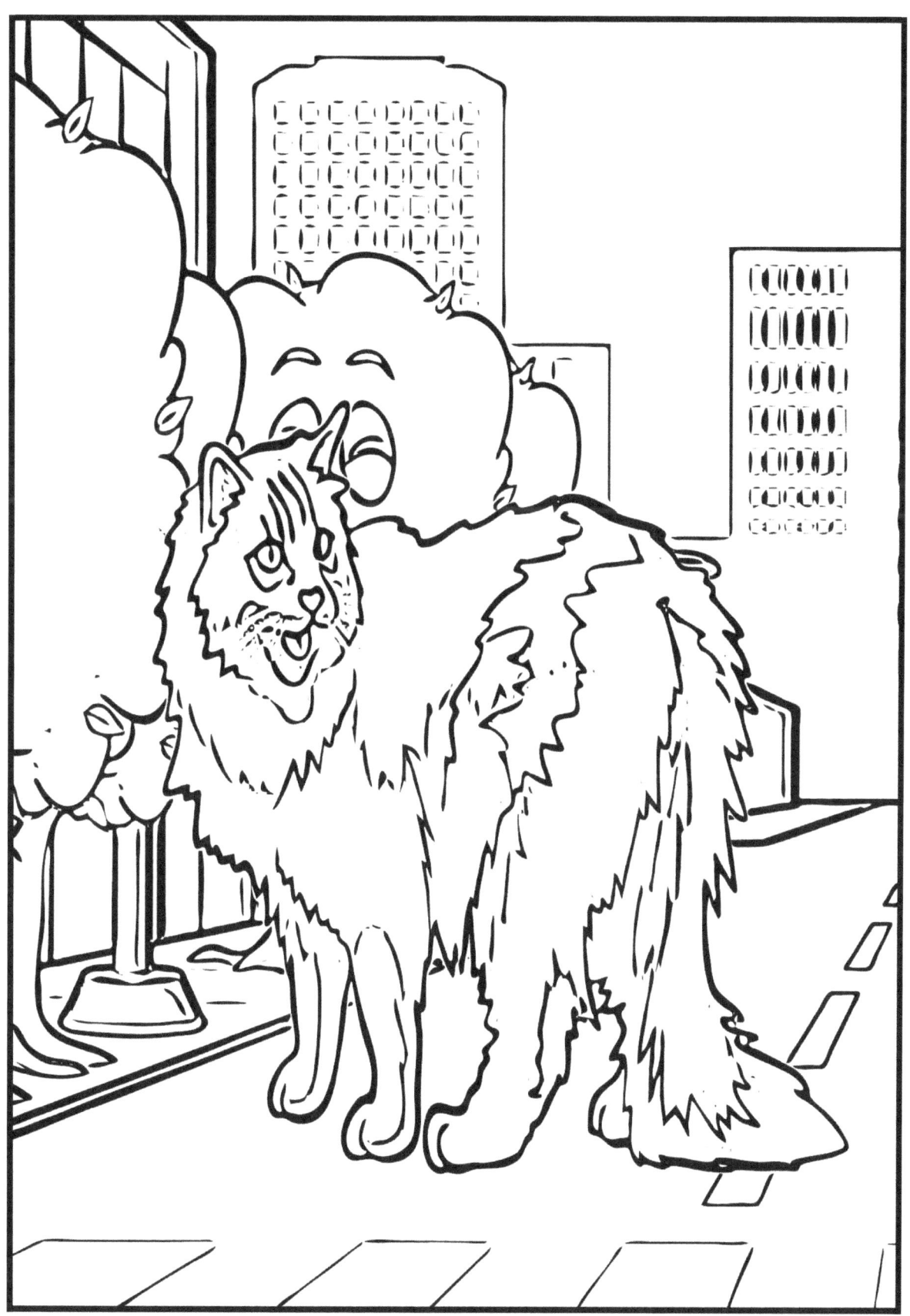

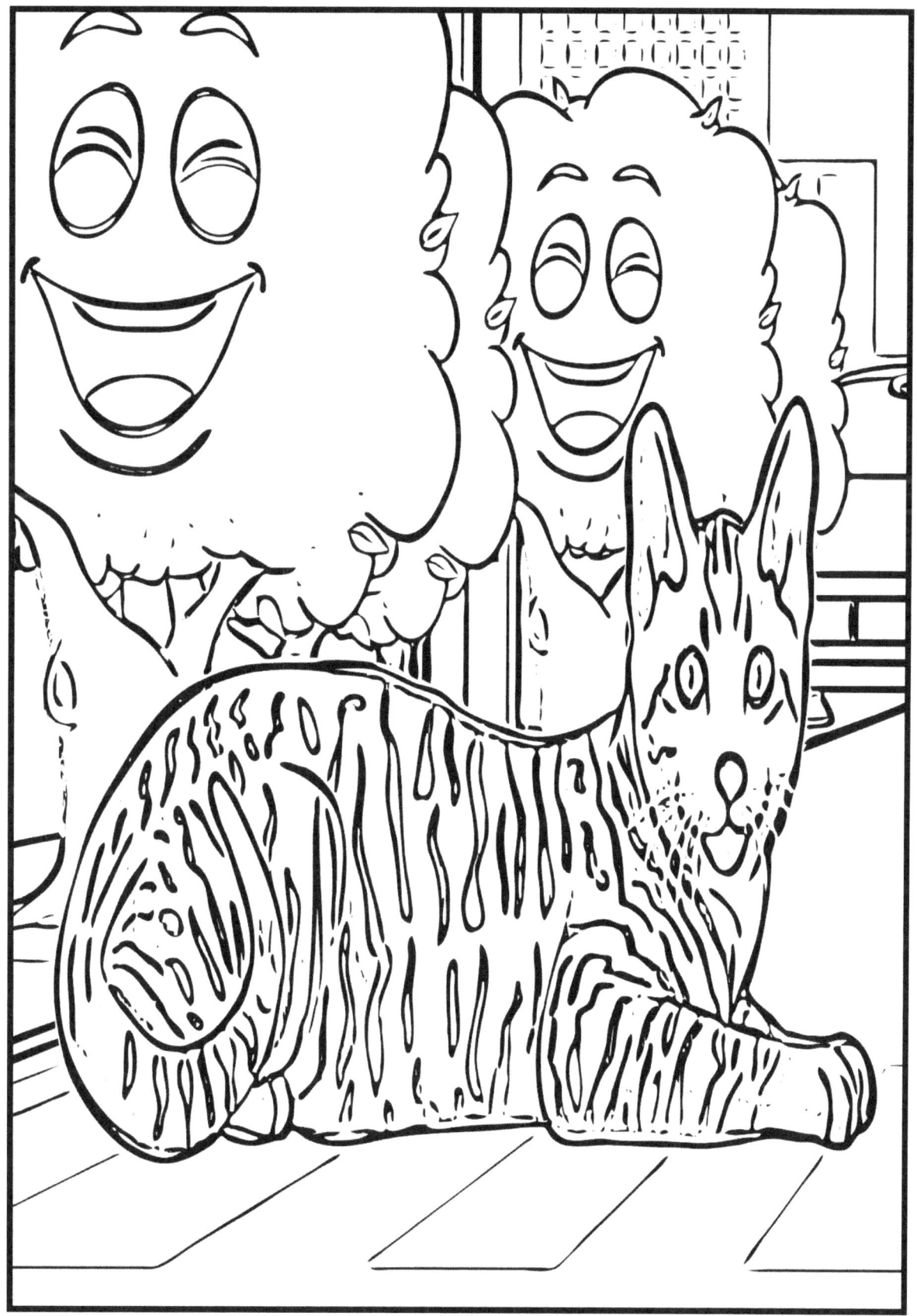

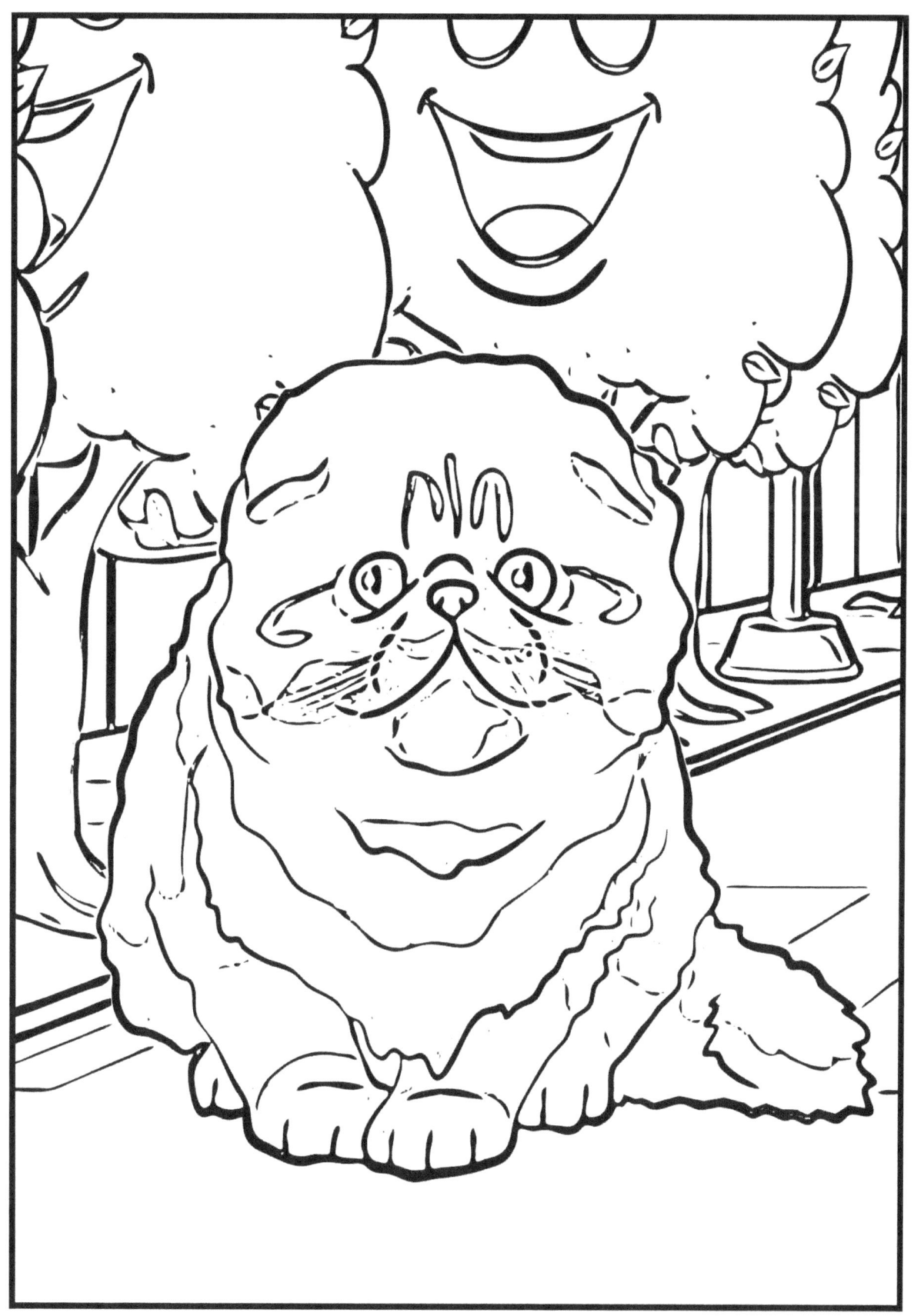

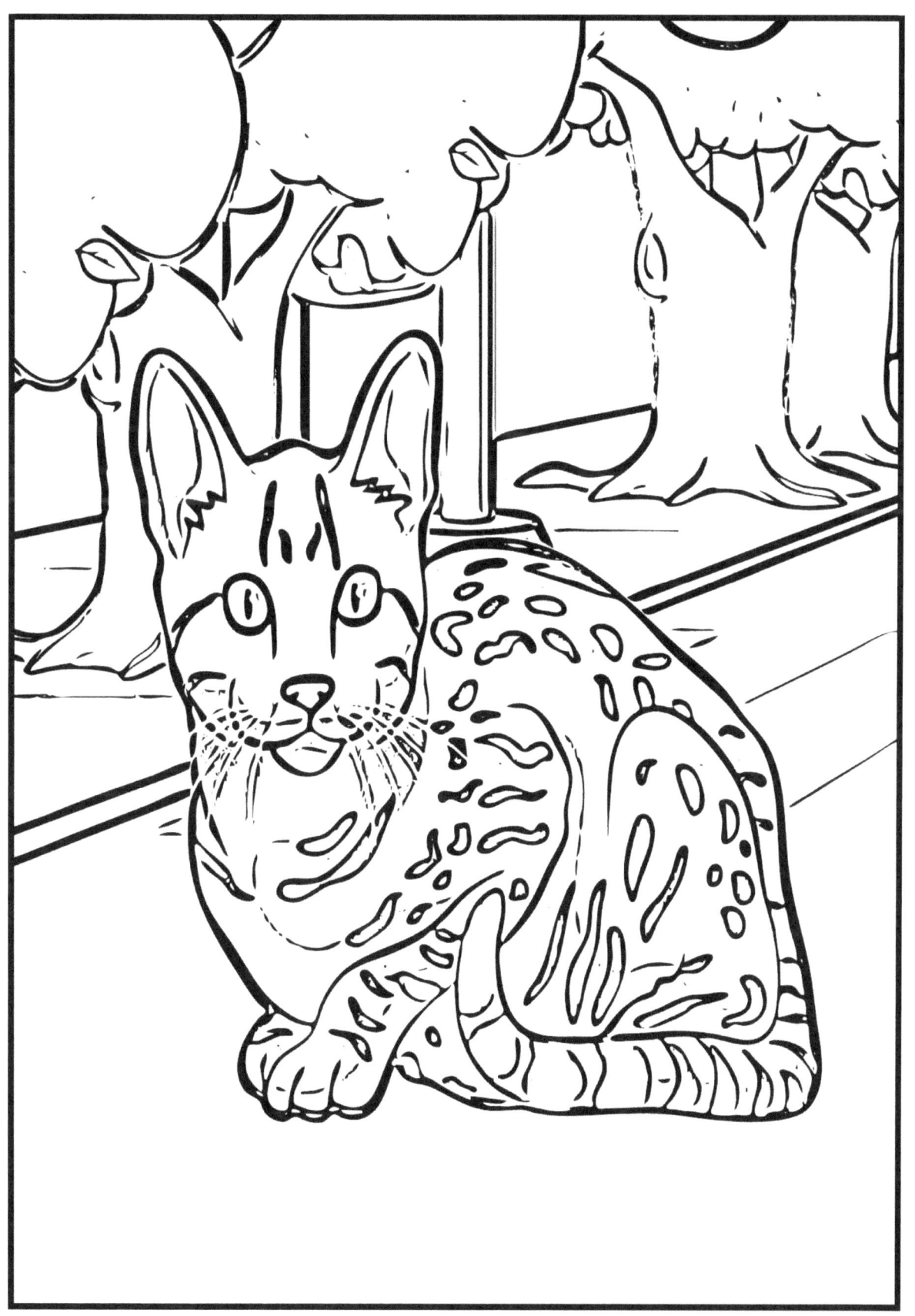

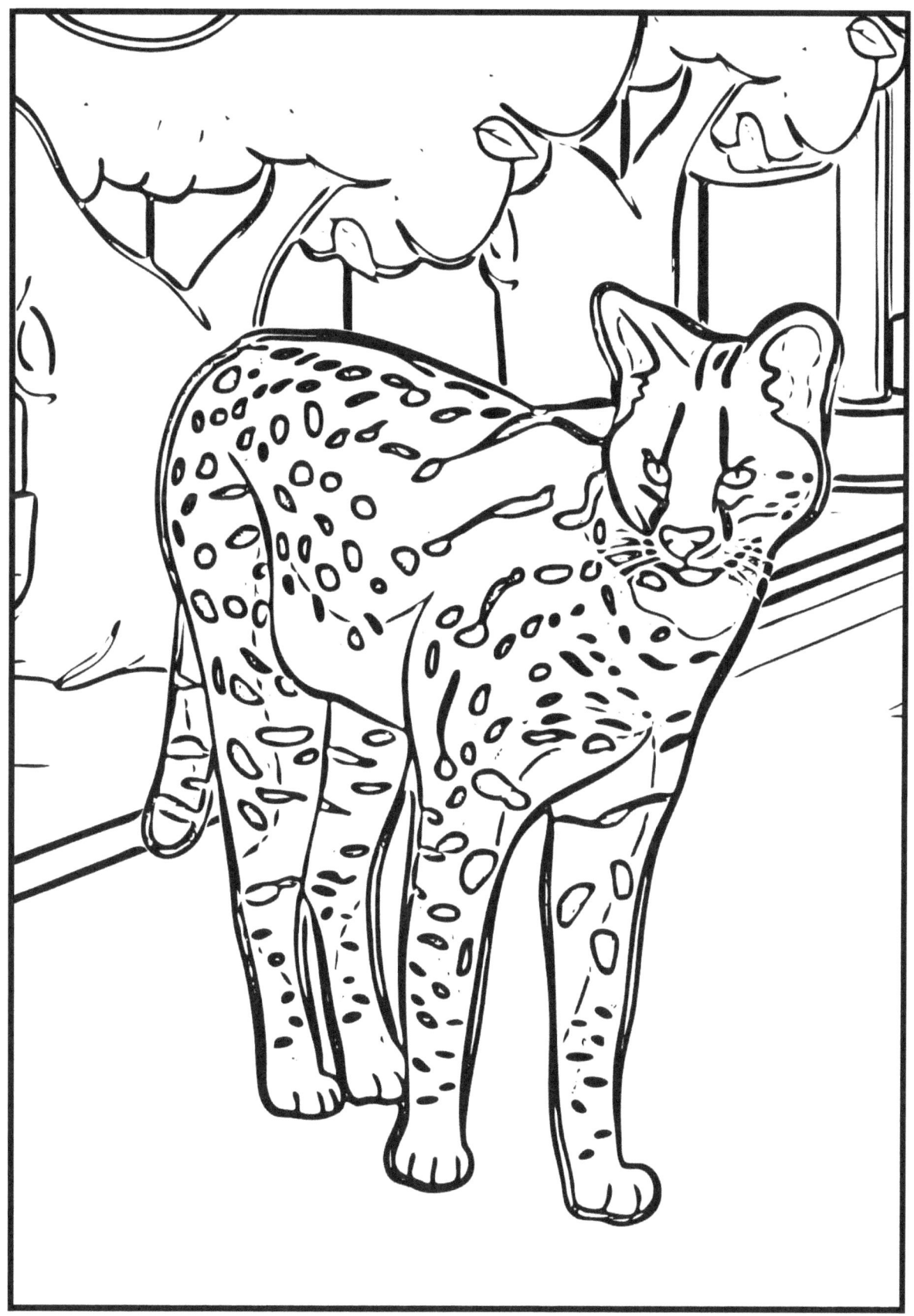

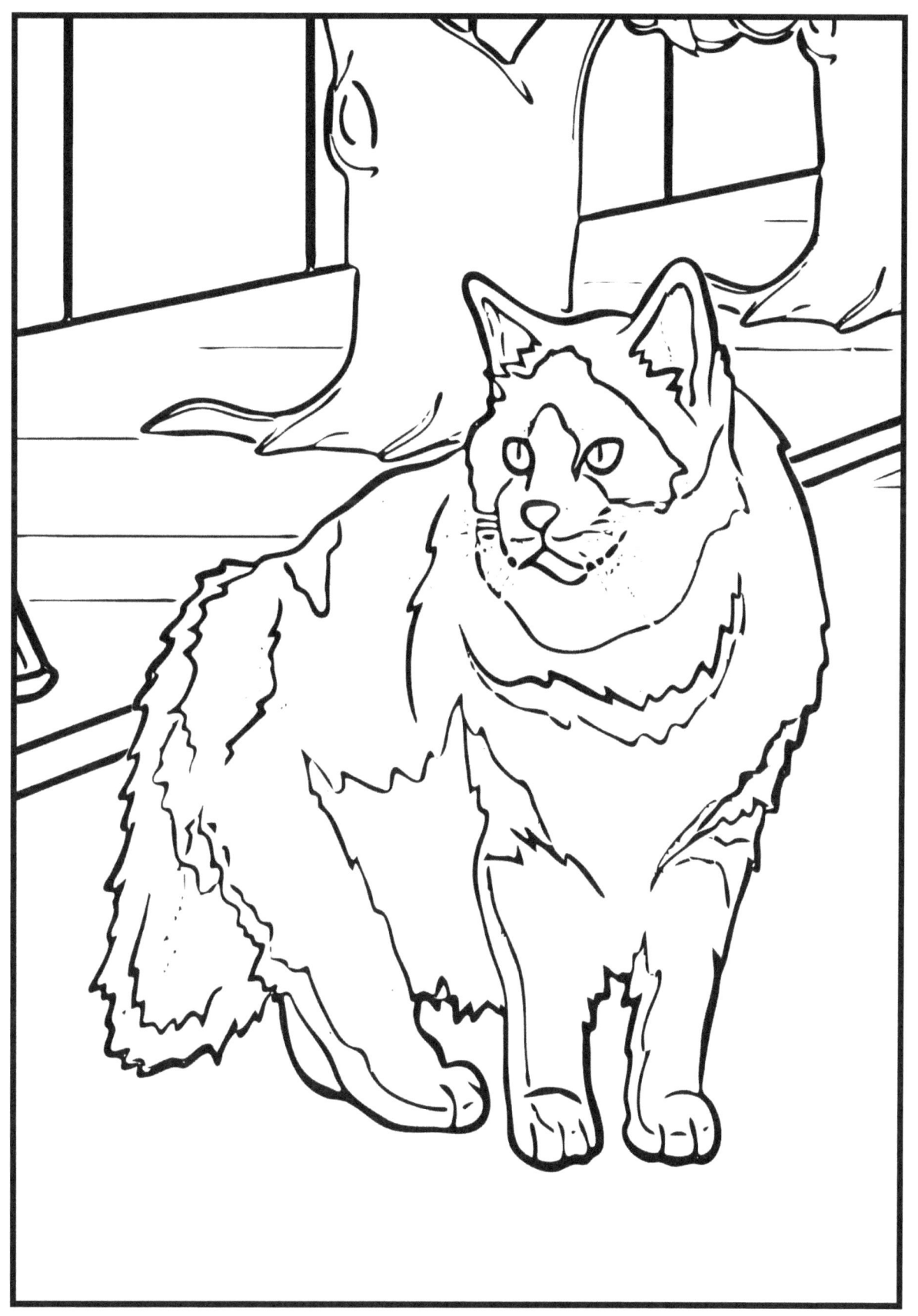

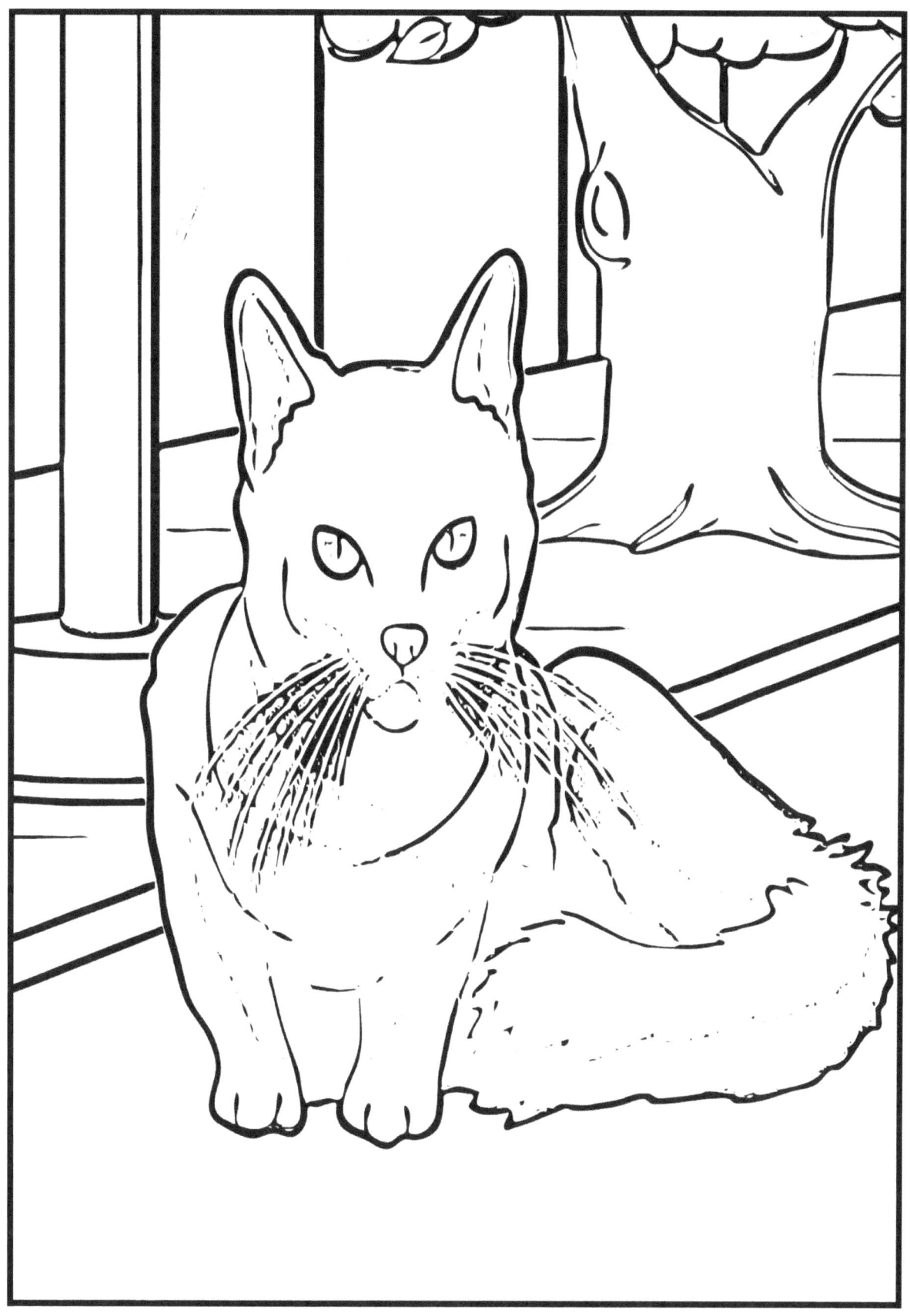

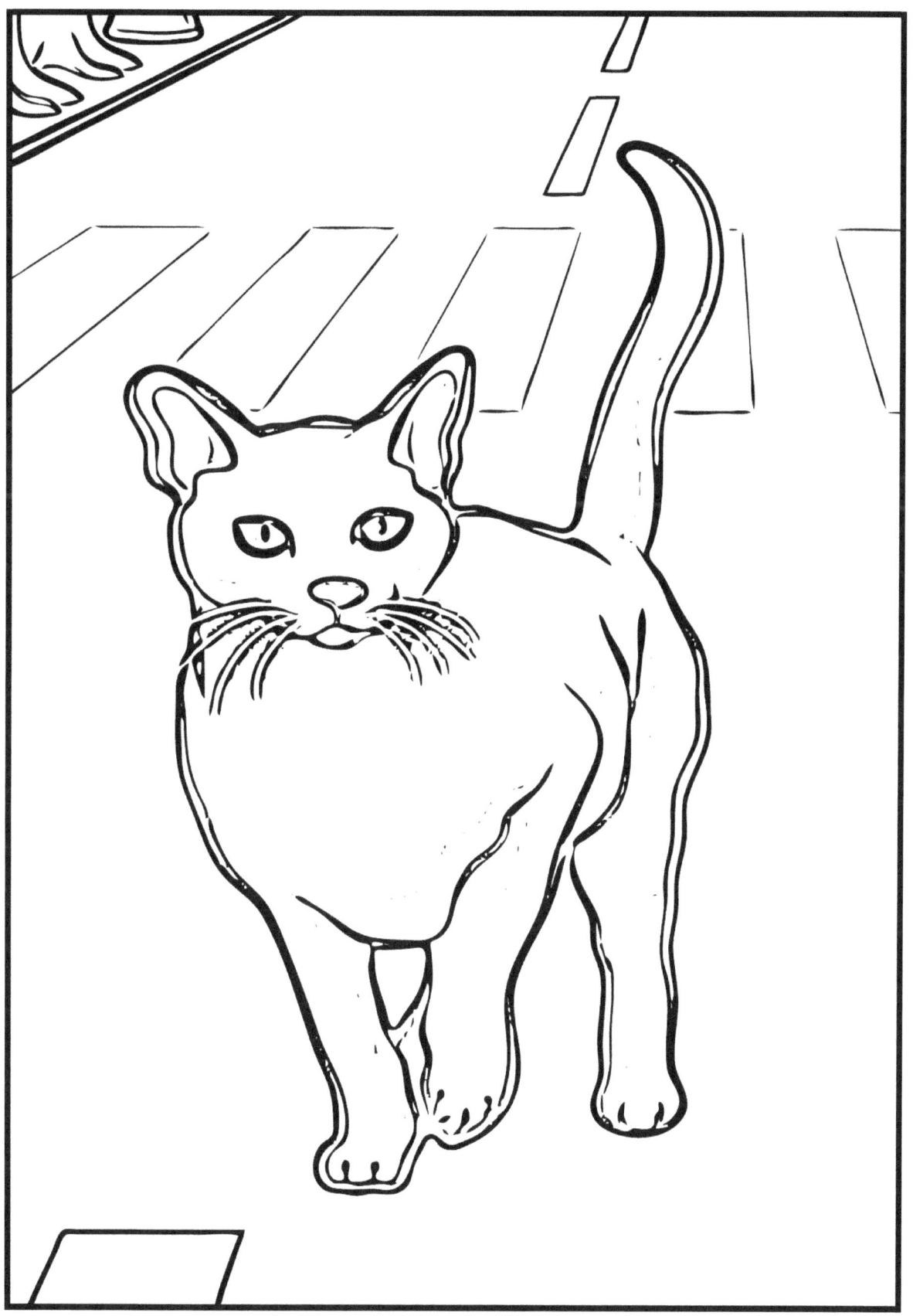

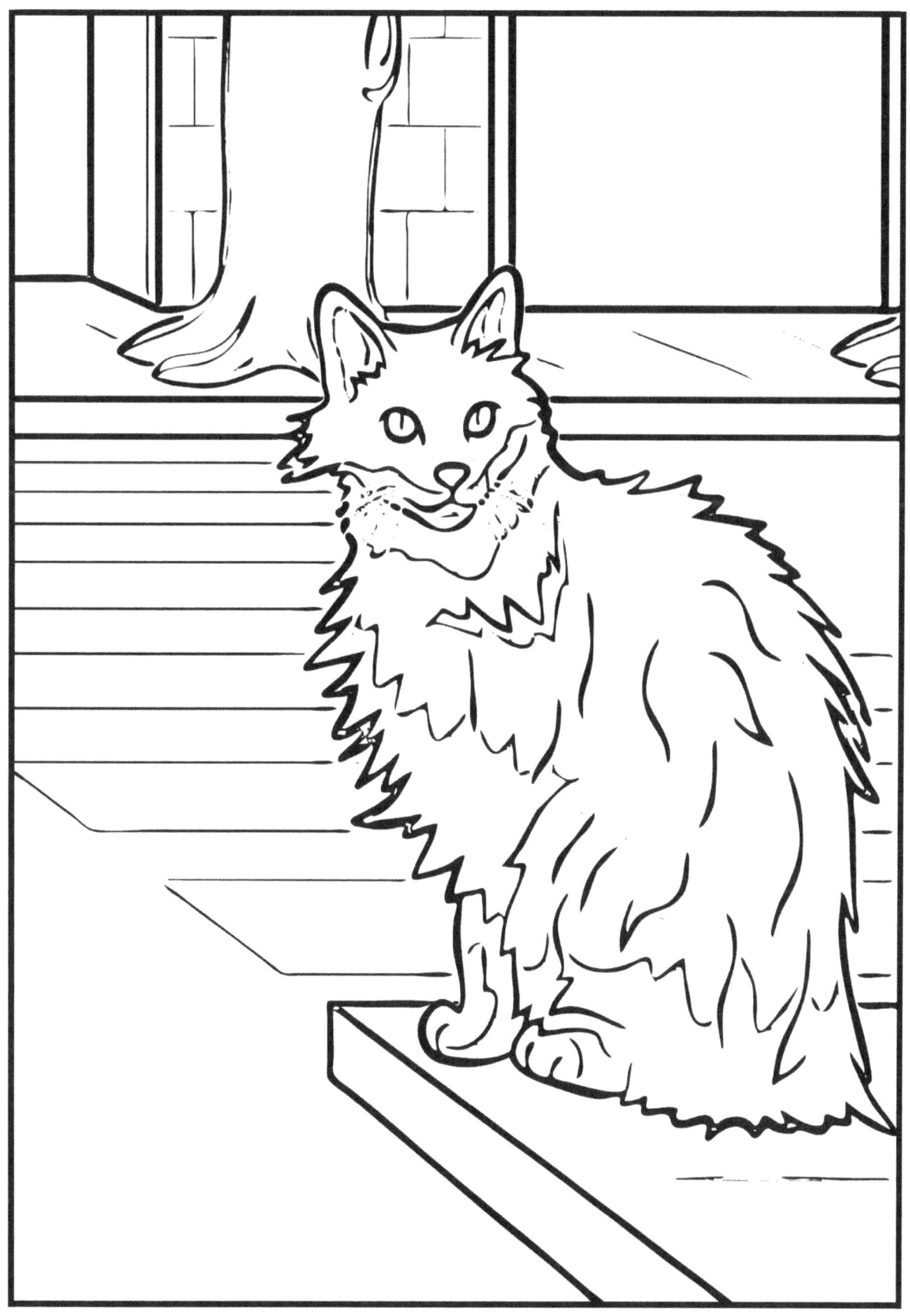

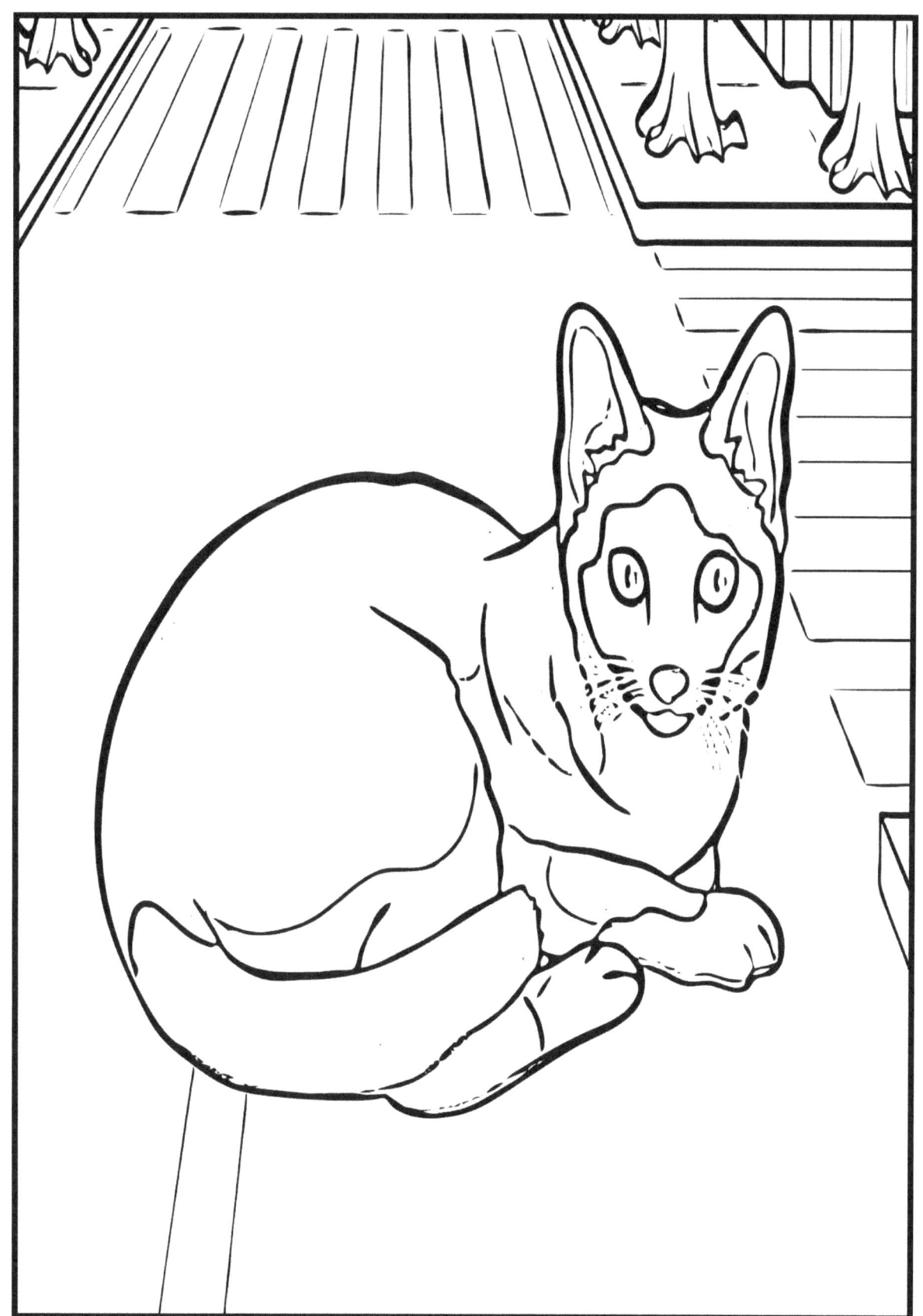

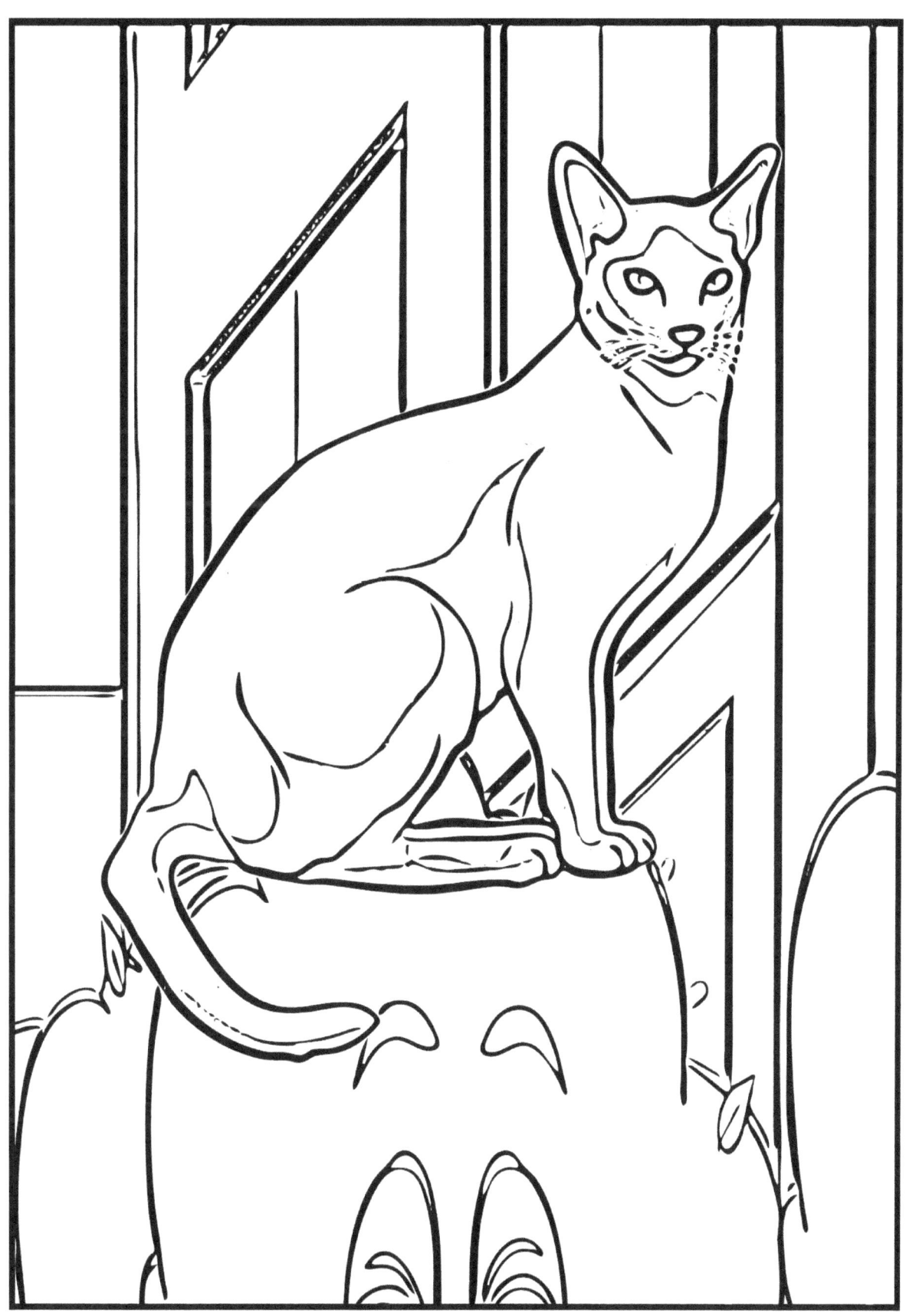

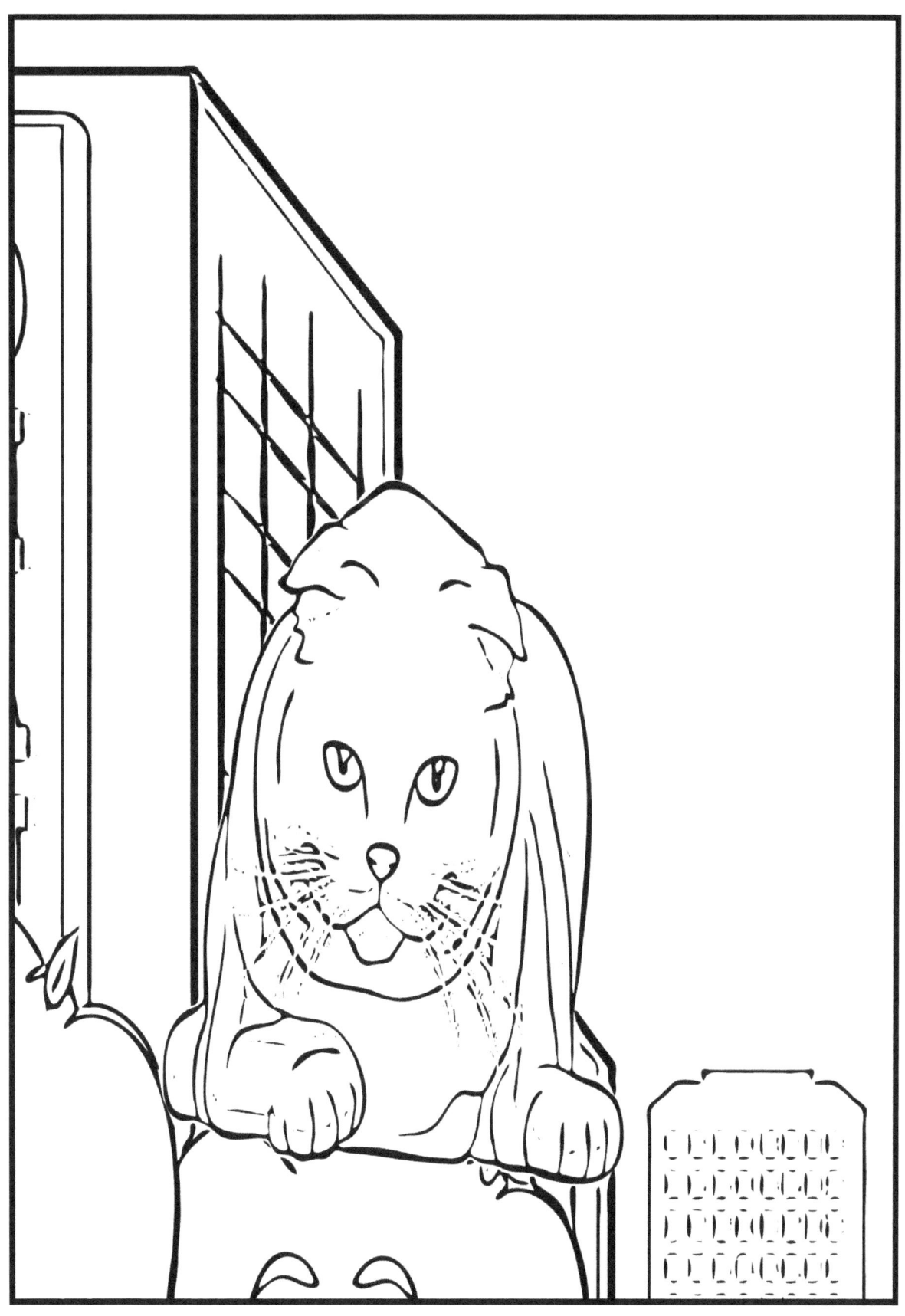

Dogs Coloring Book For Adults
BIG DOGS
Fantasy Art Coloring Book For Stress Relief

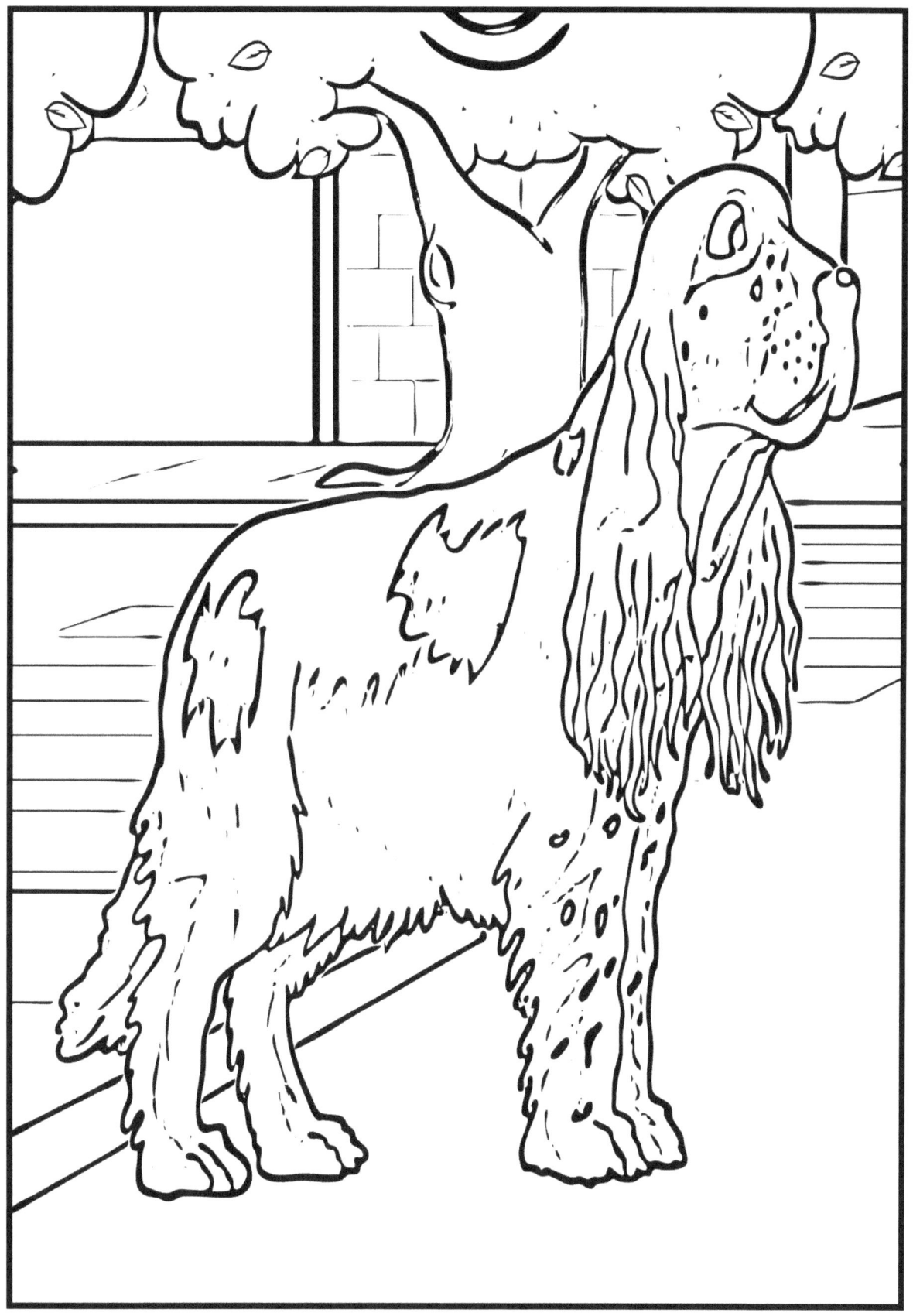

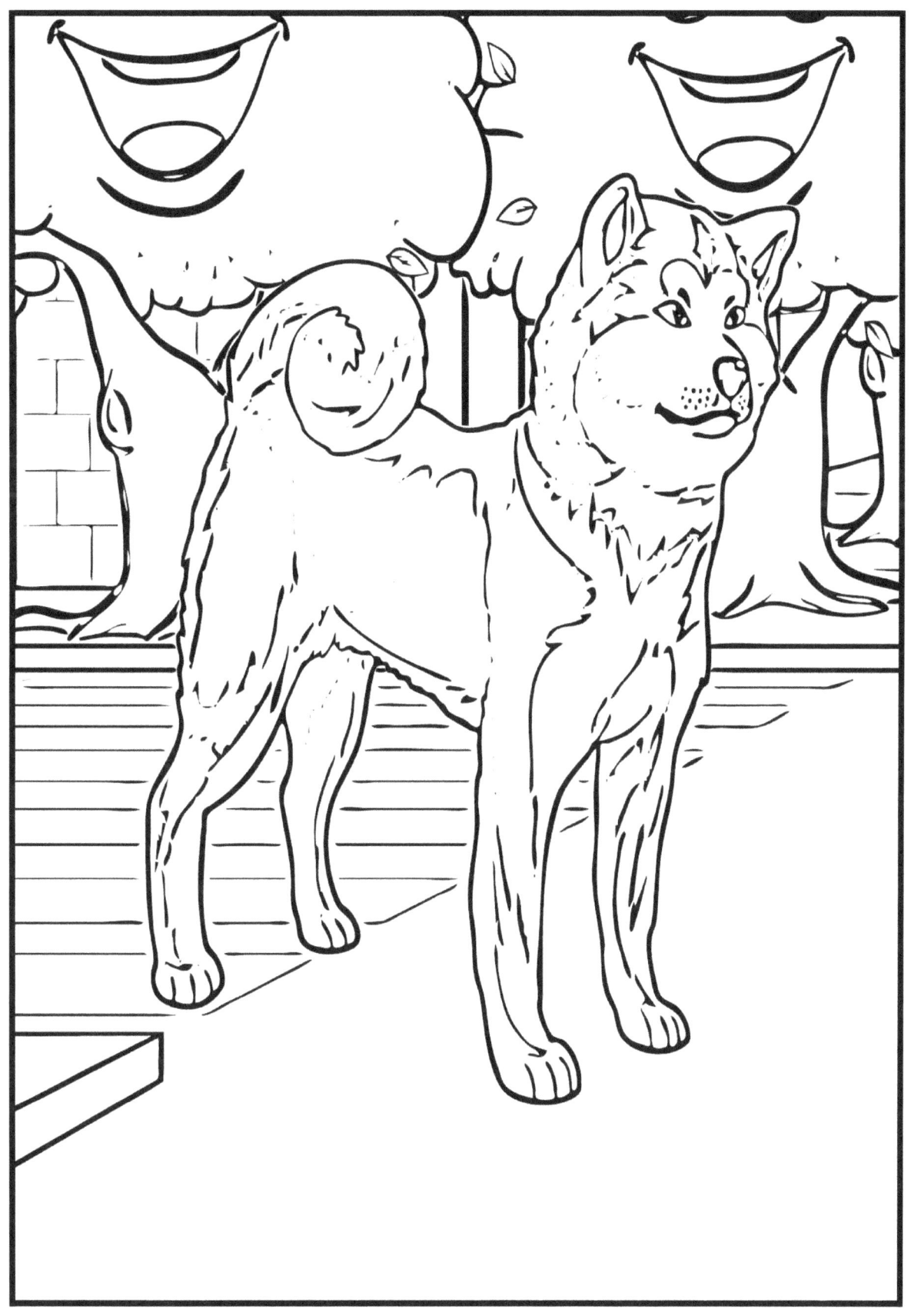

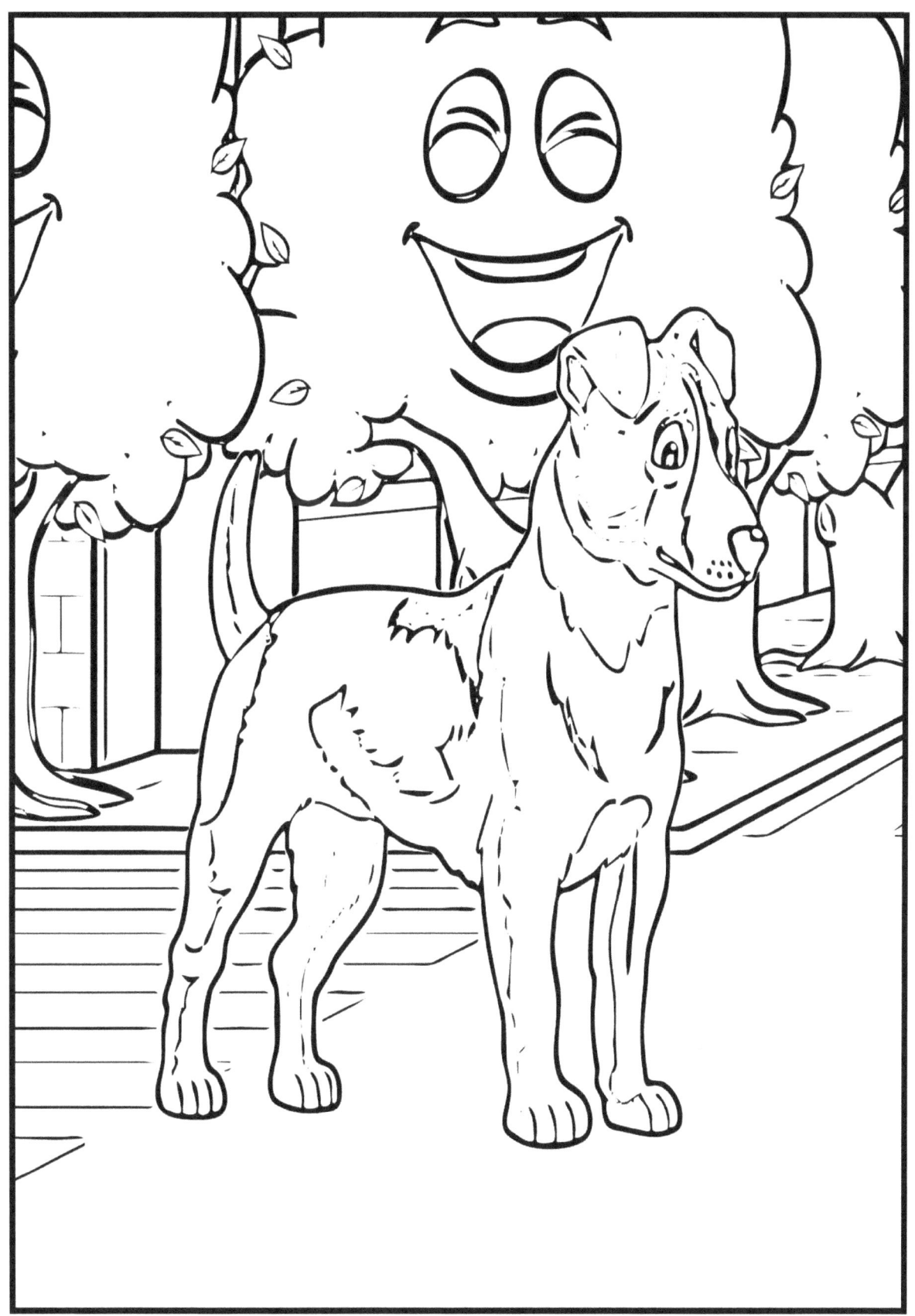

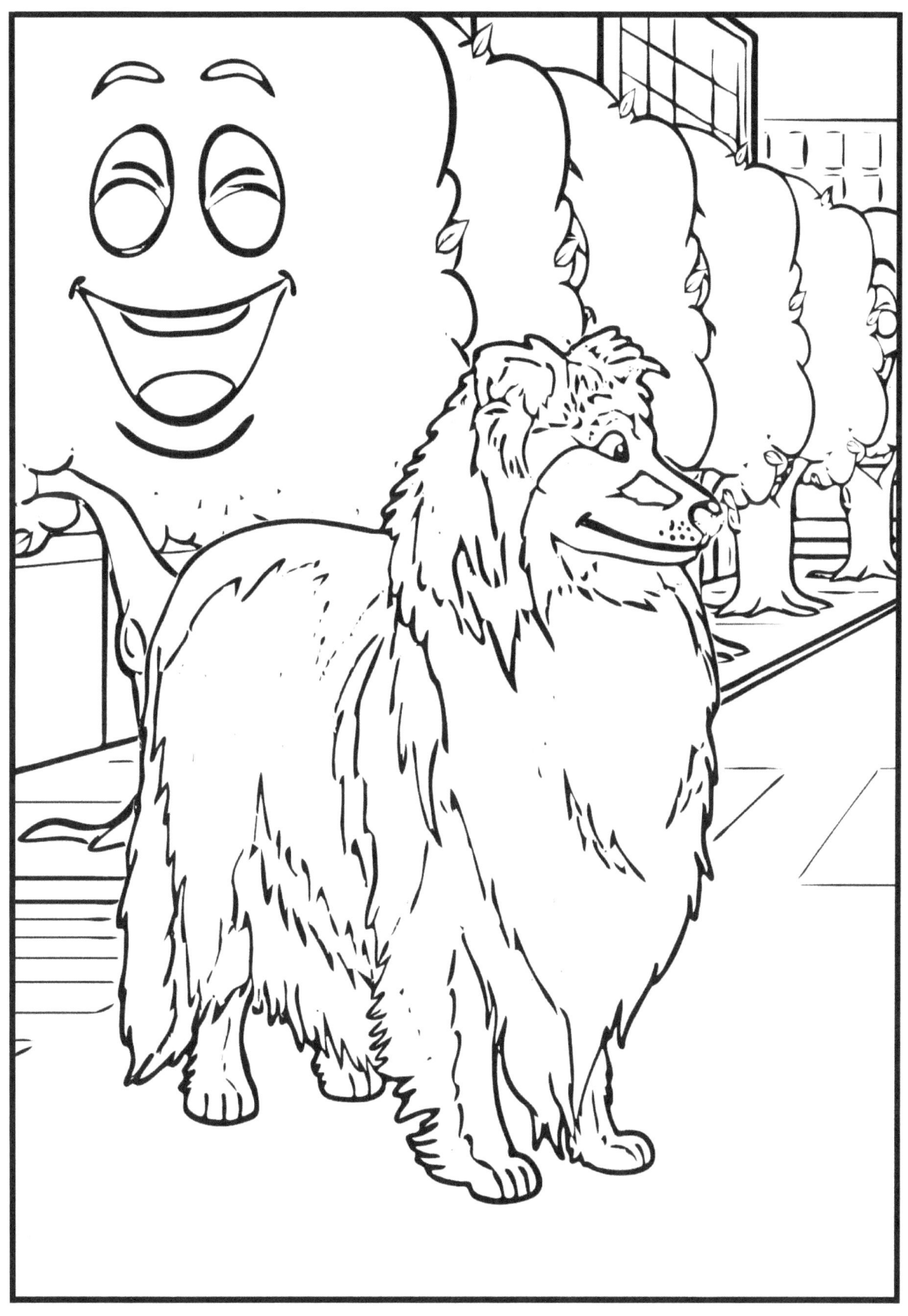

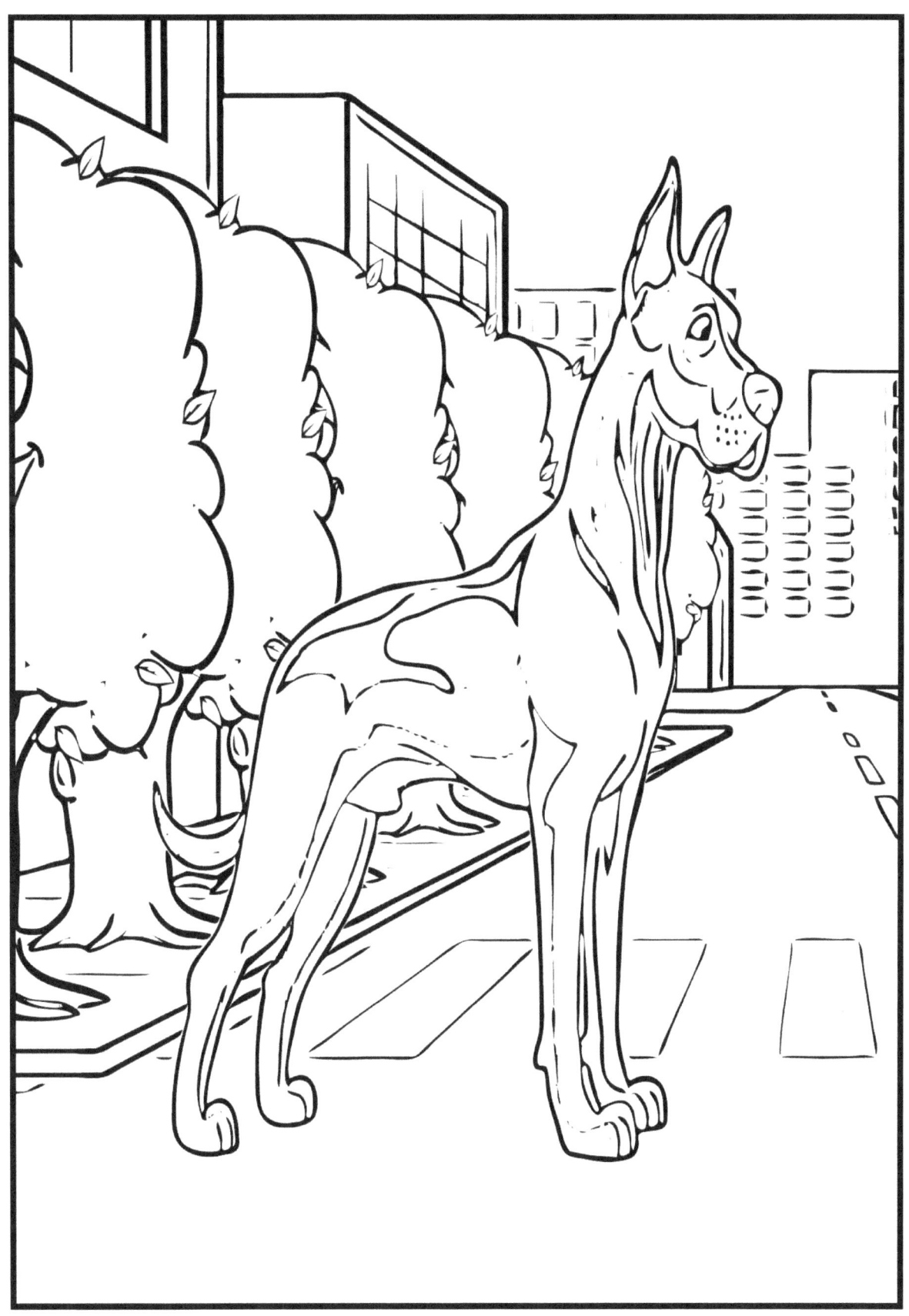

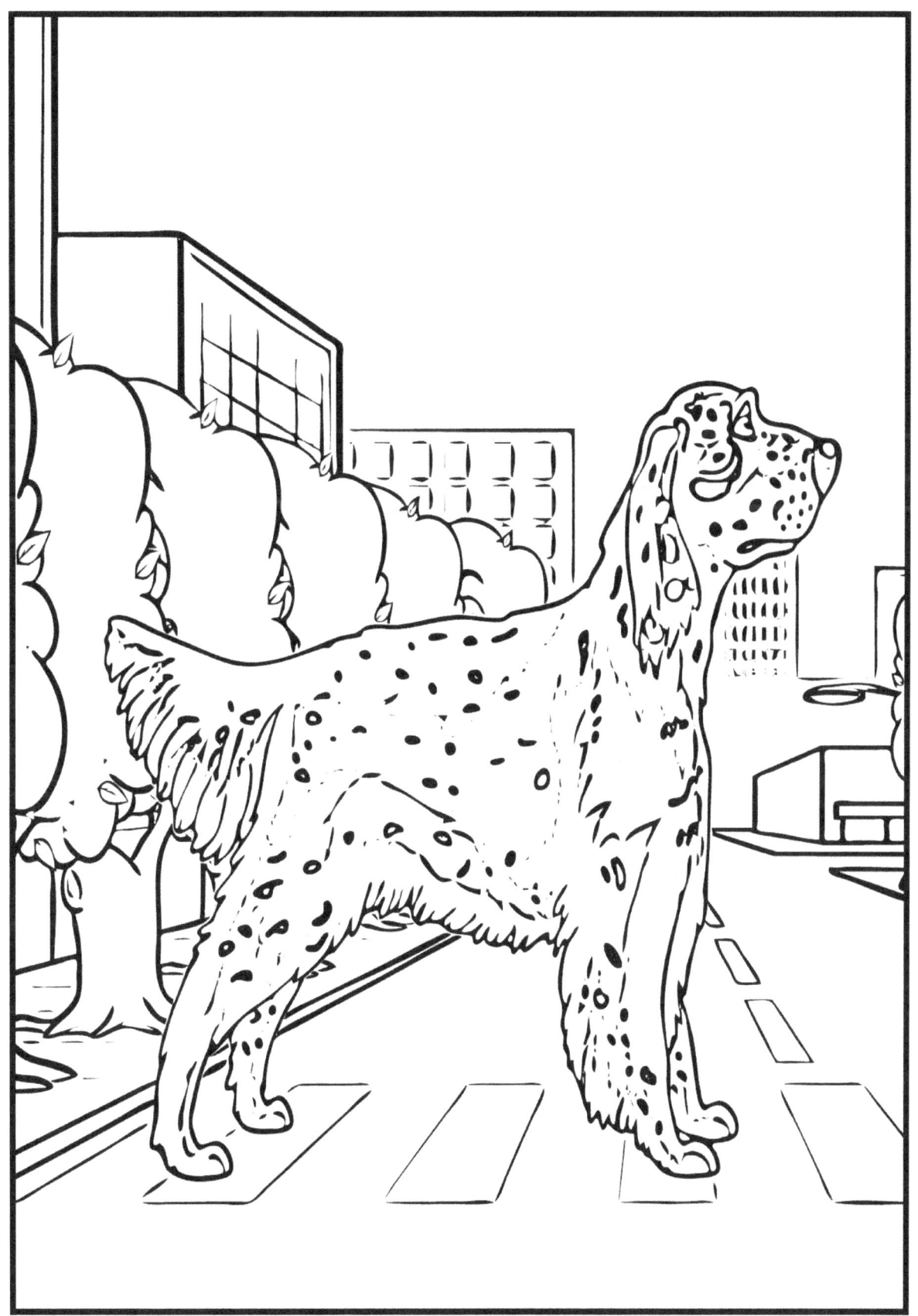

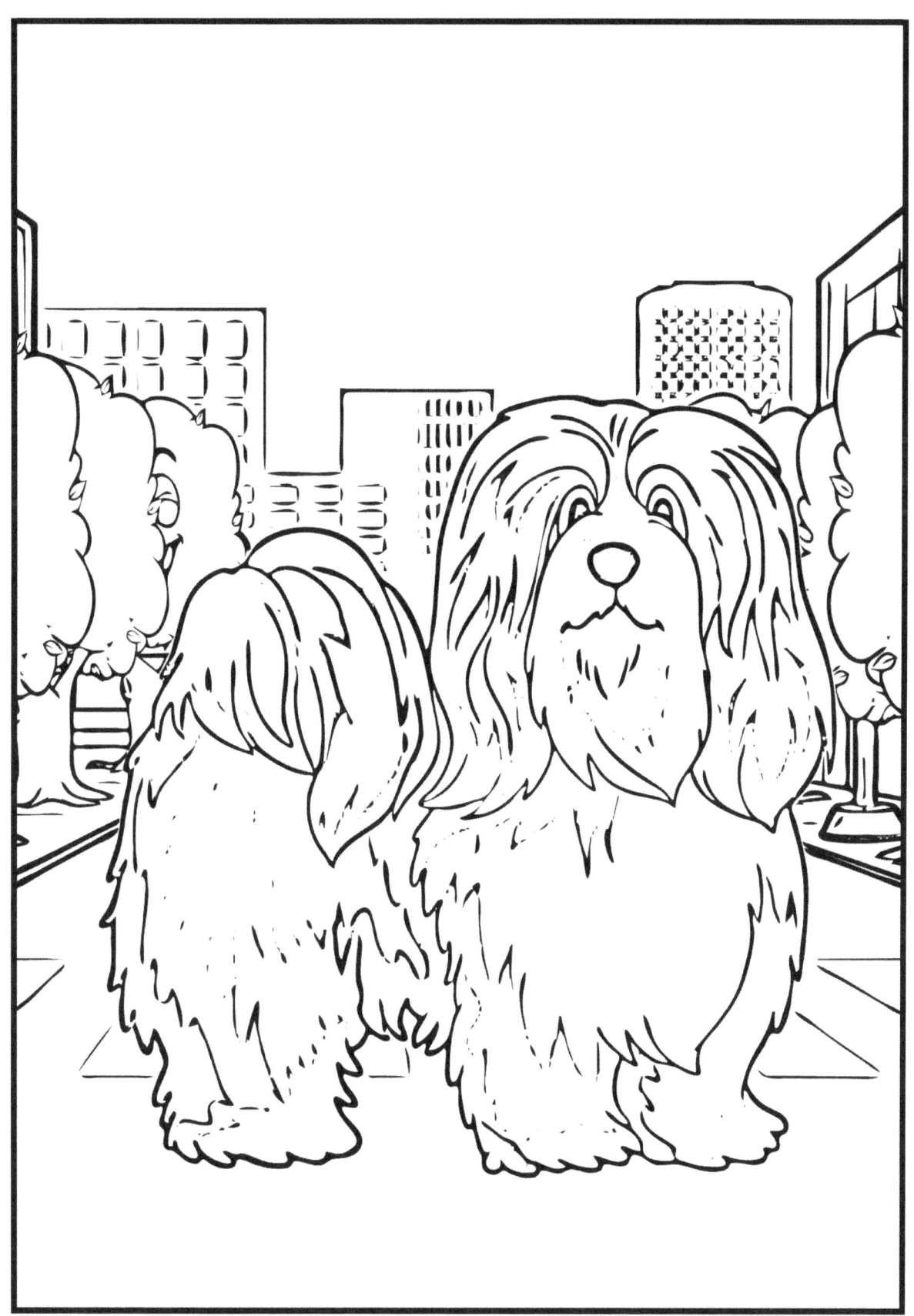

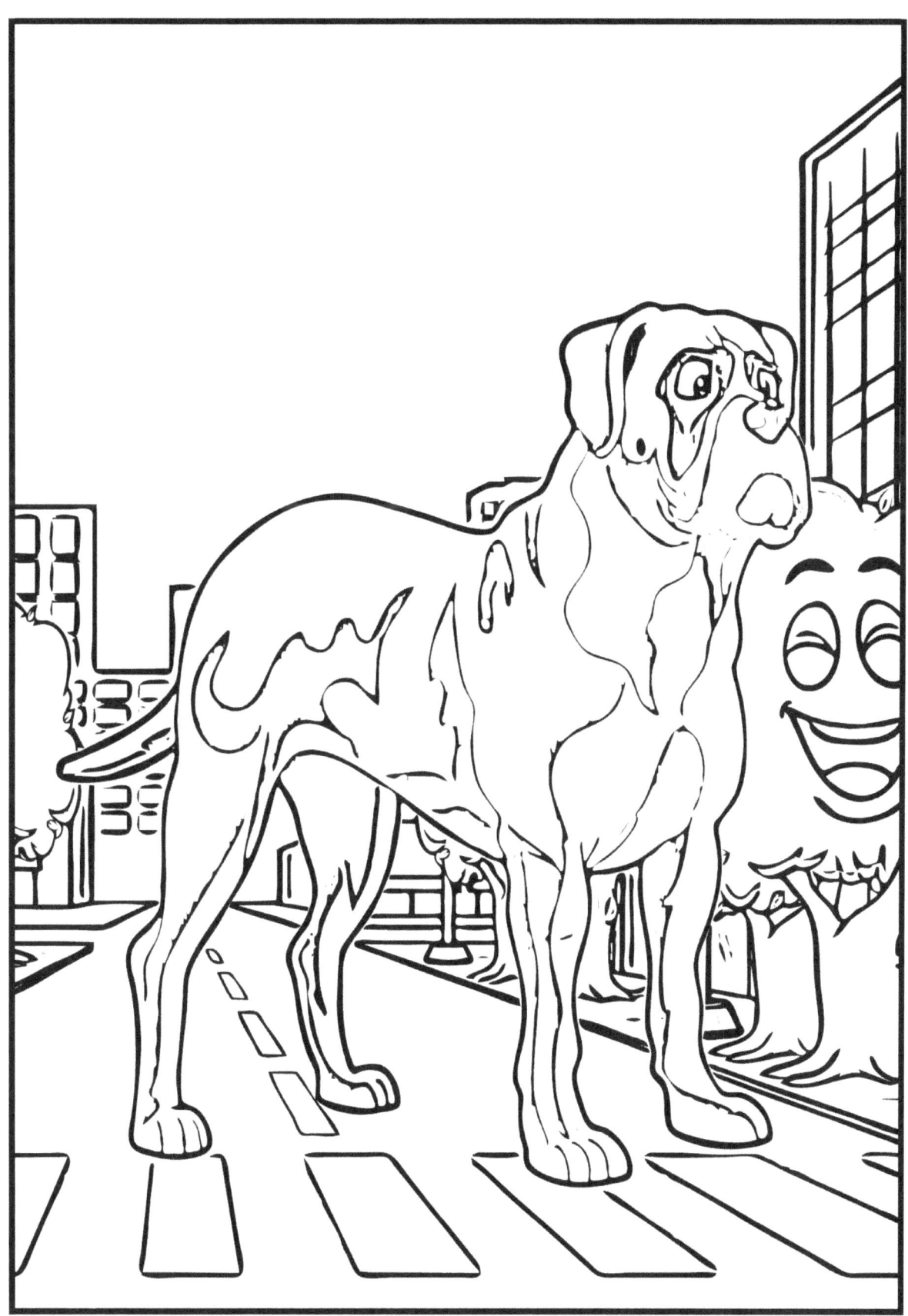

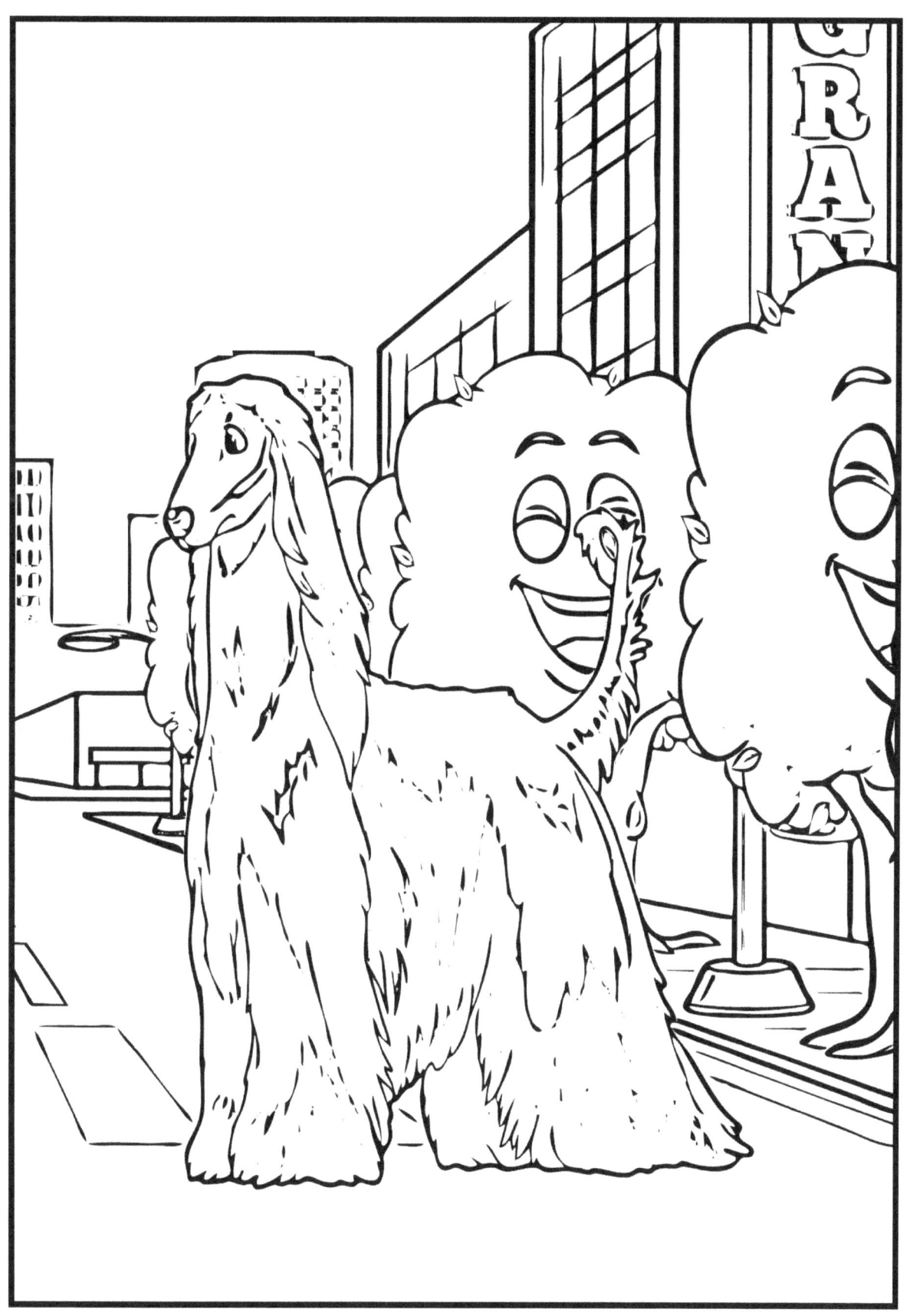

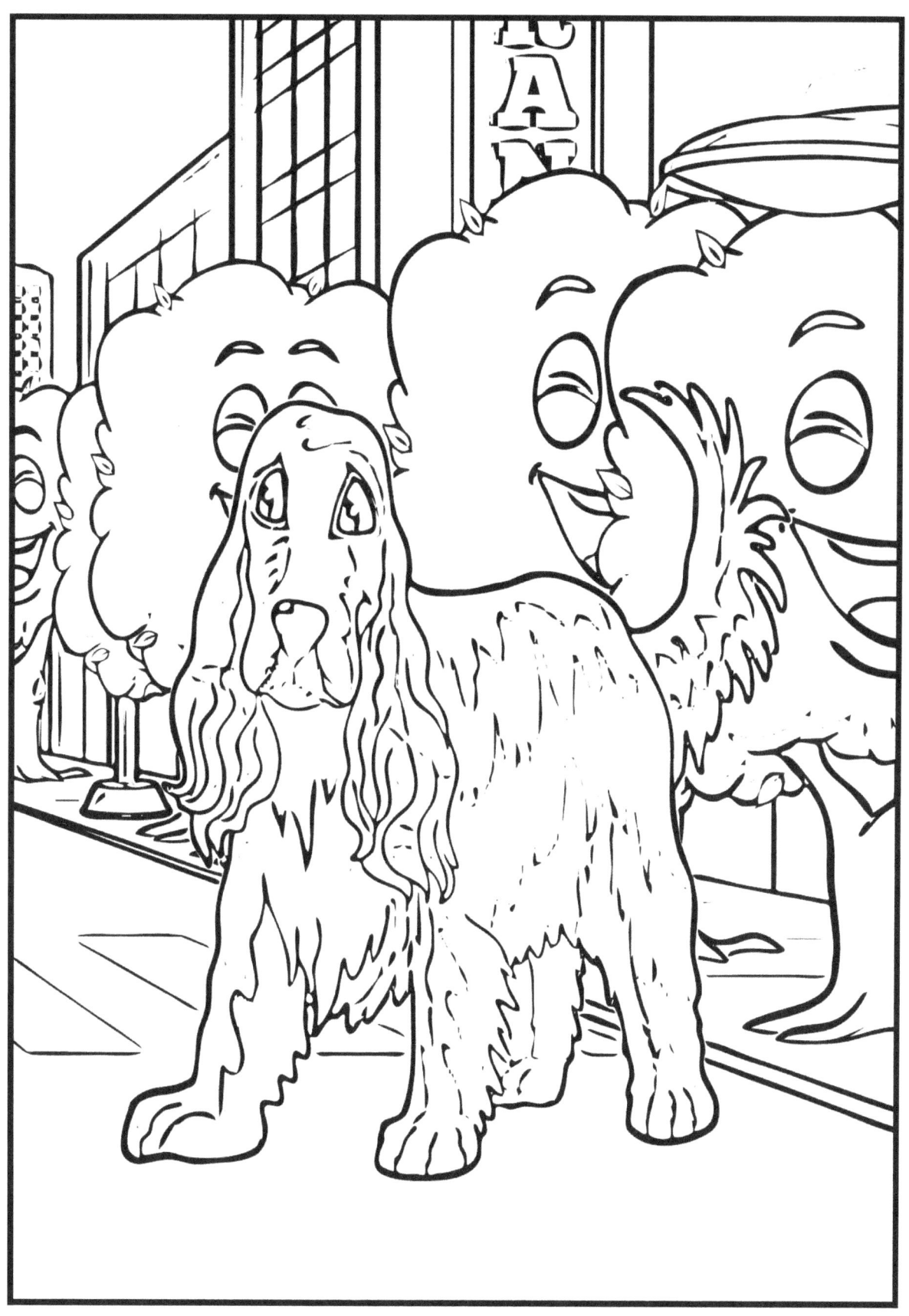

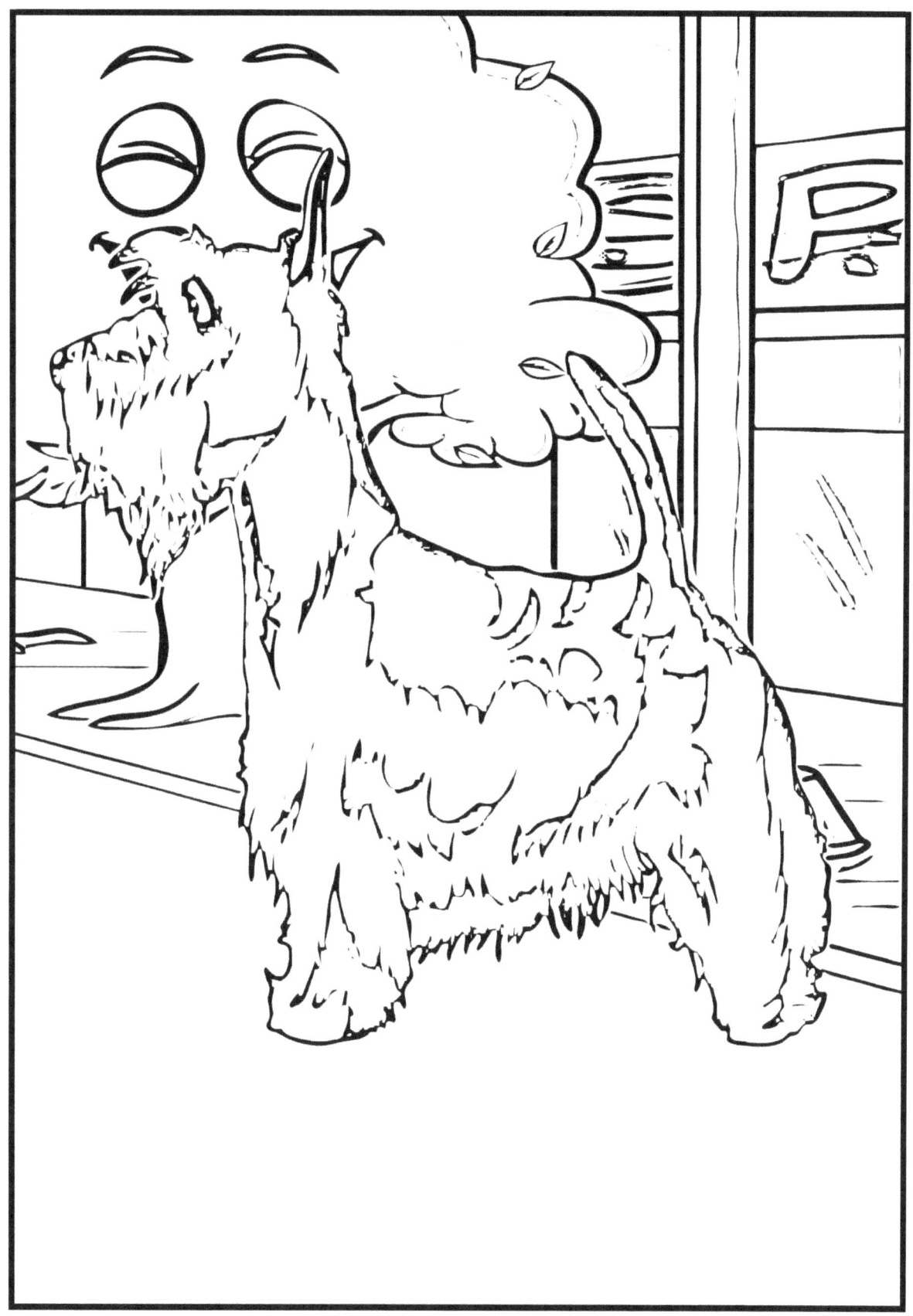

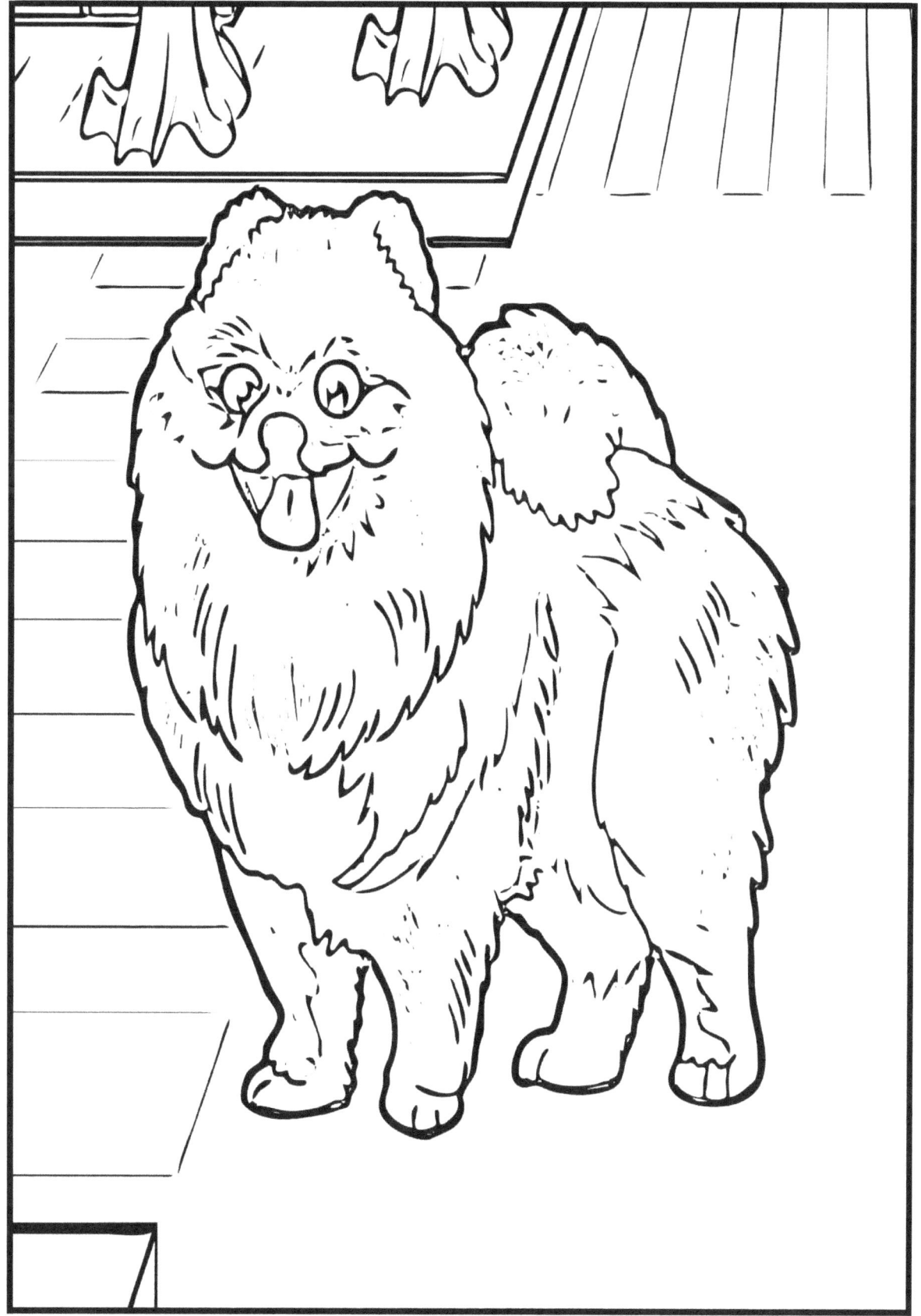

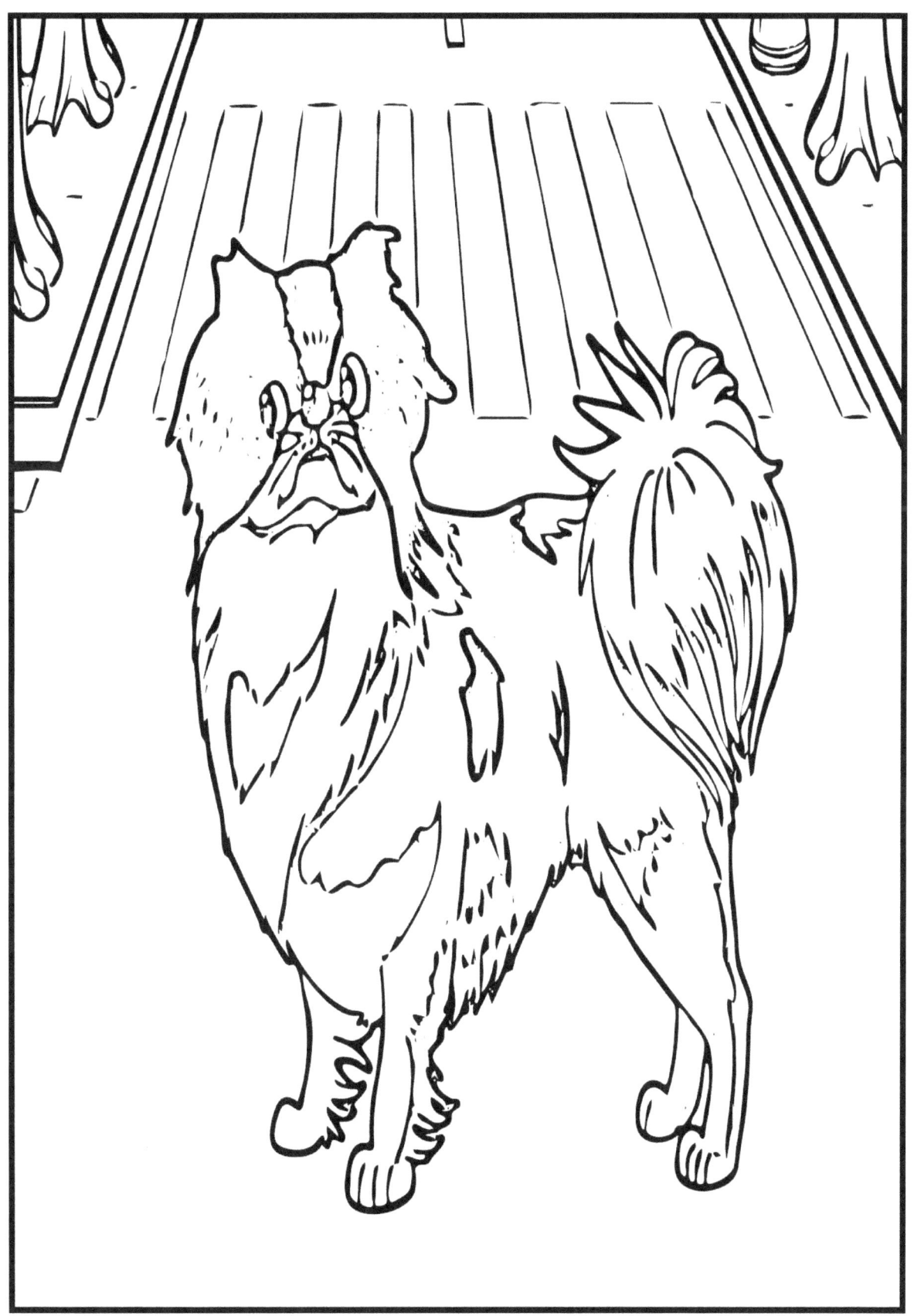

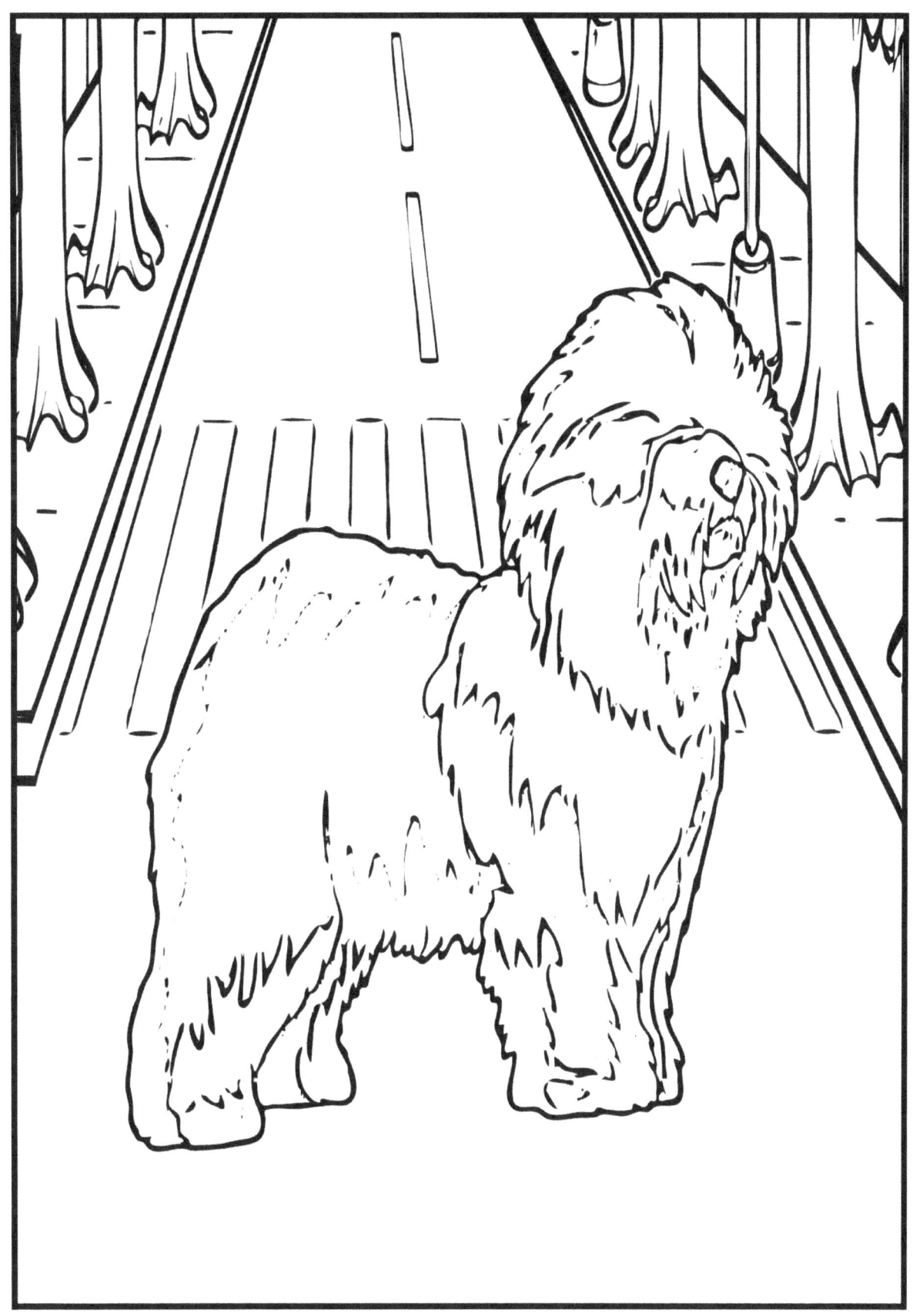

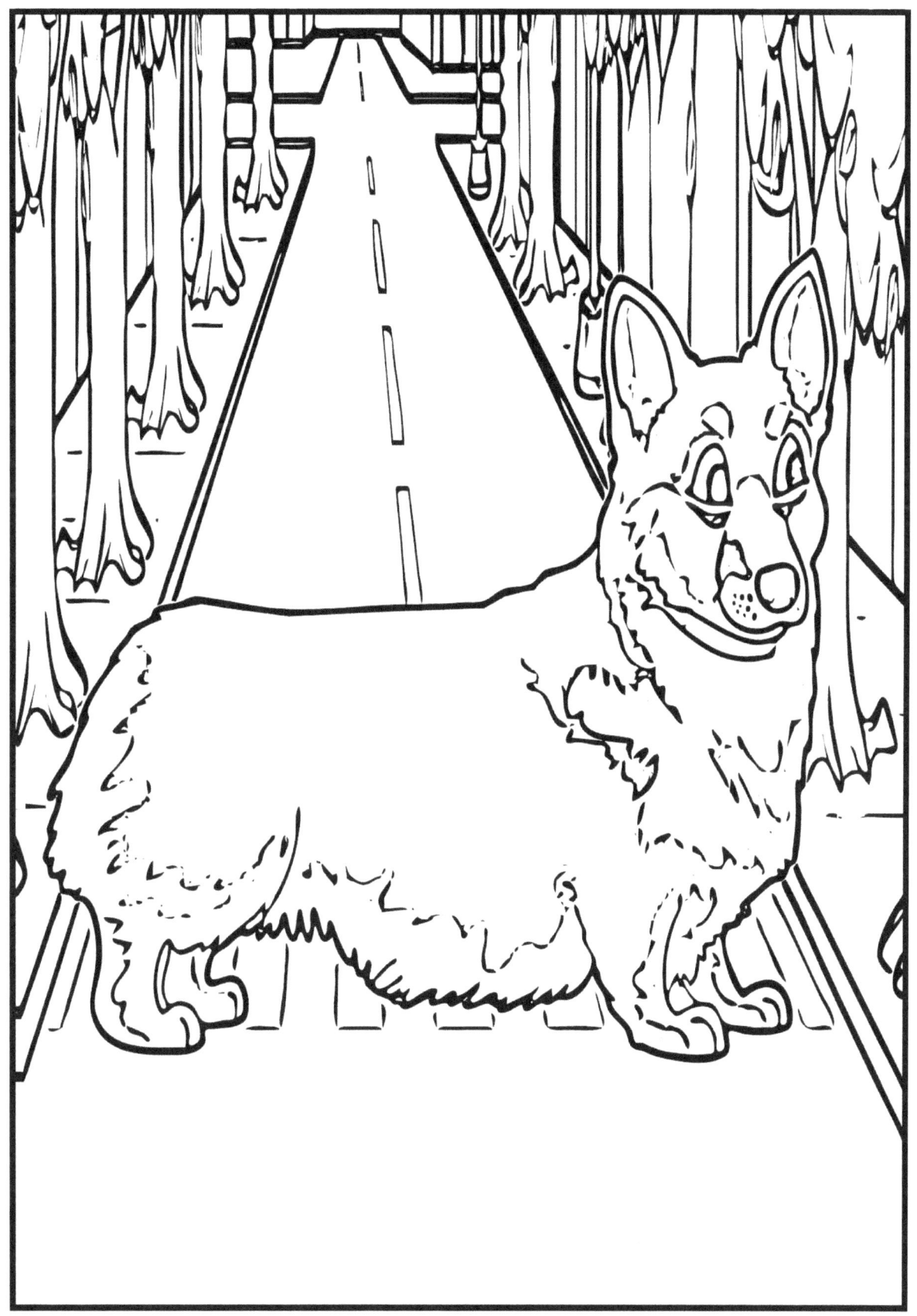

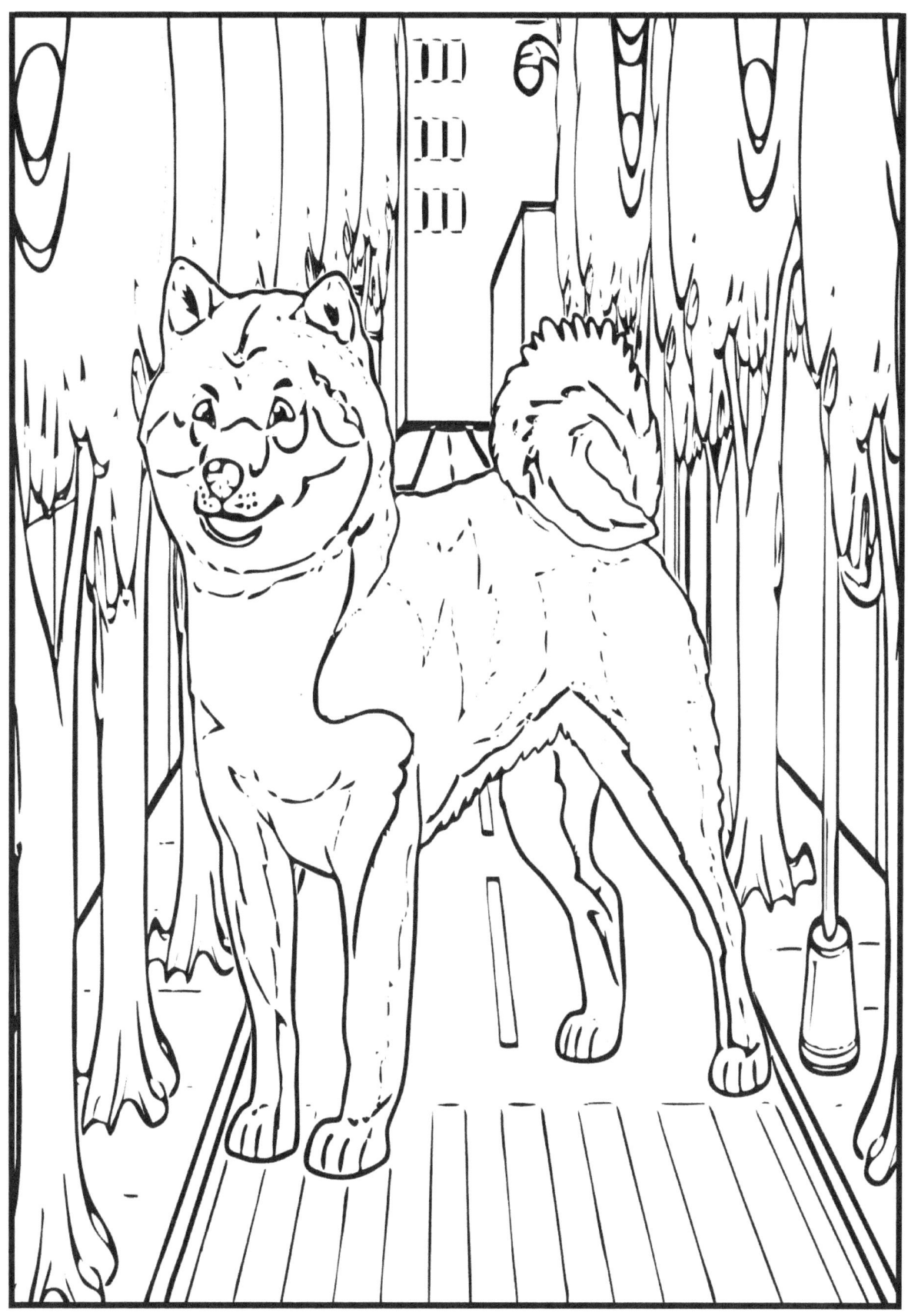

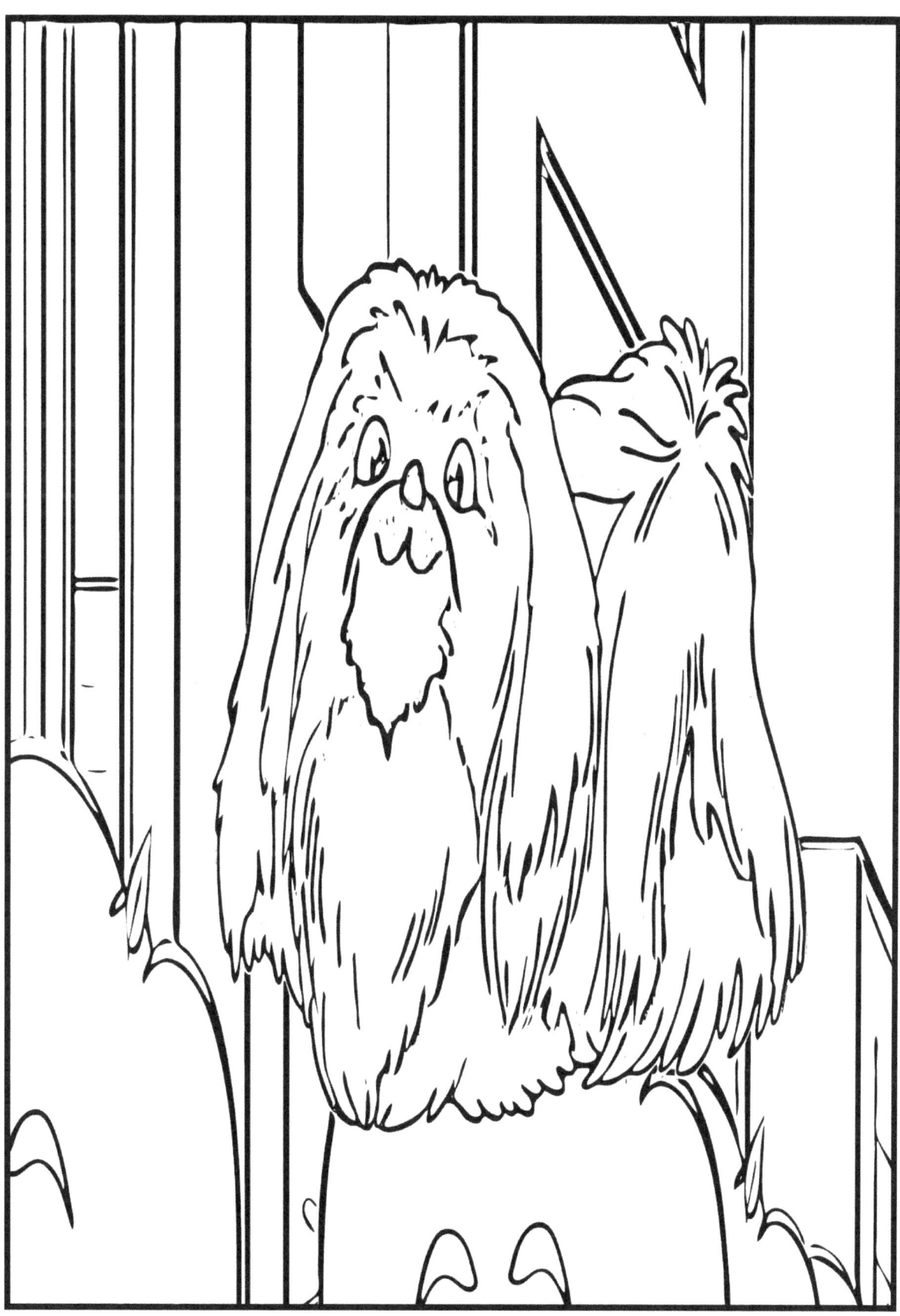

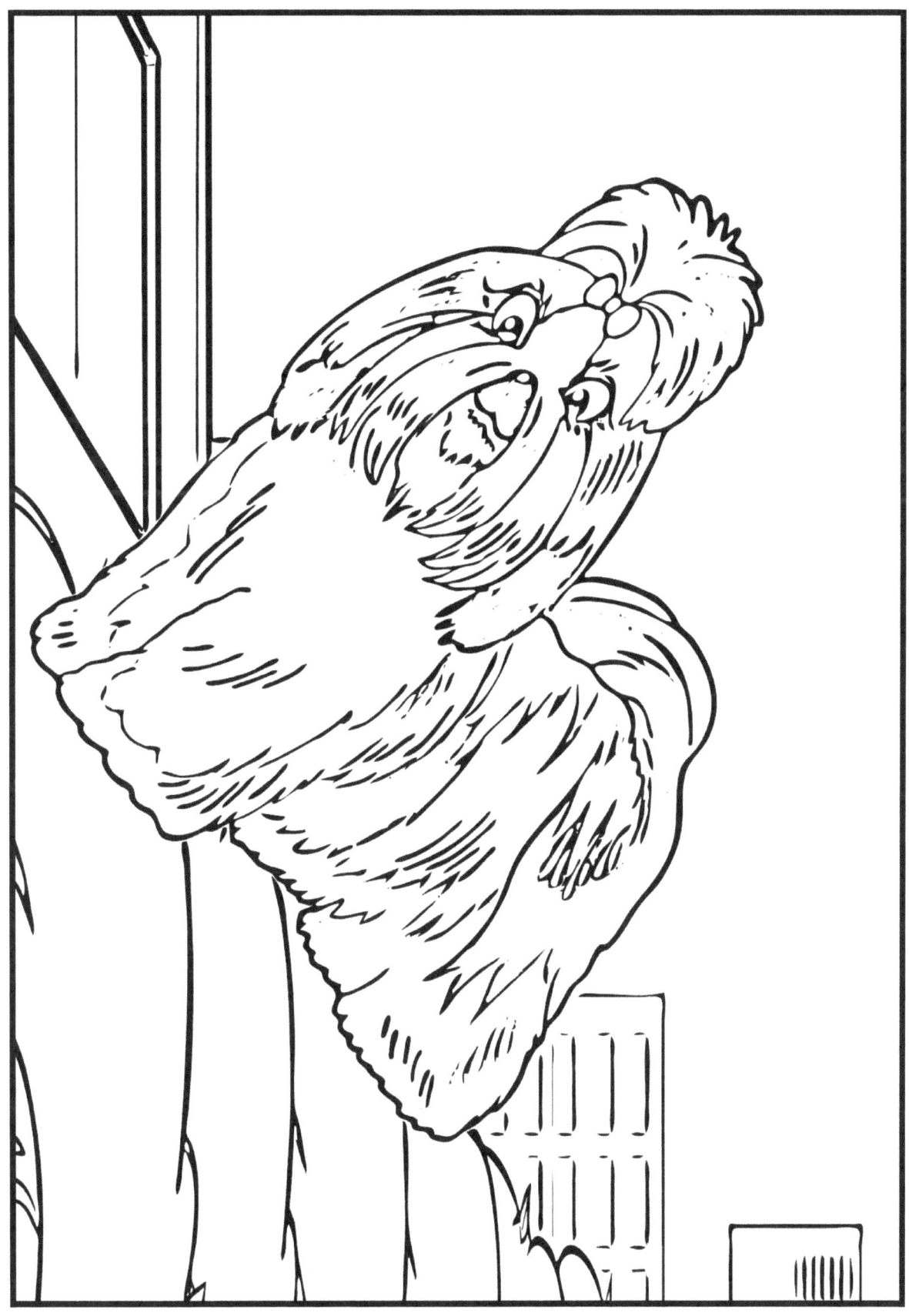

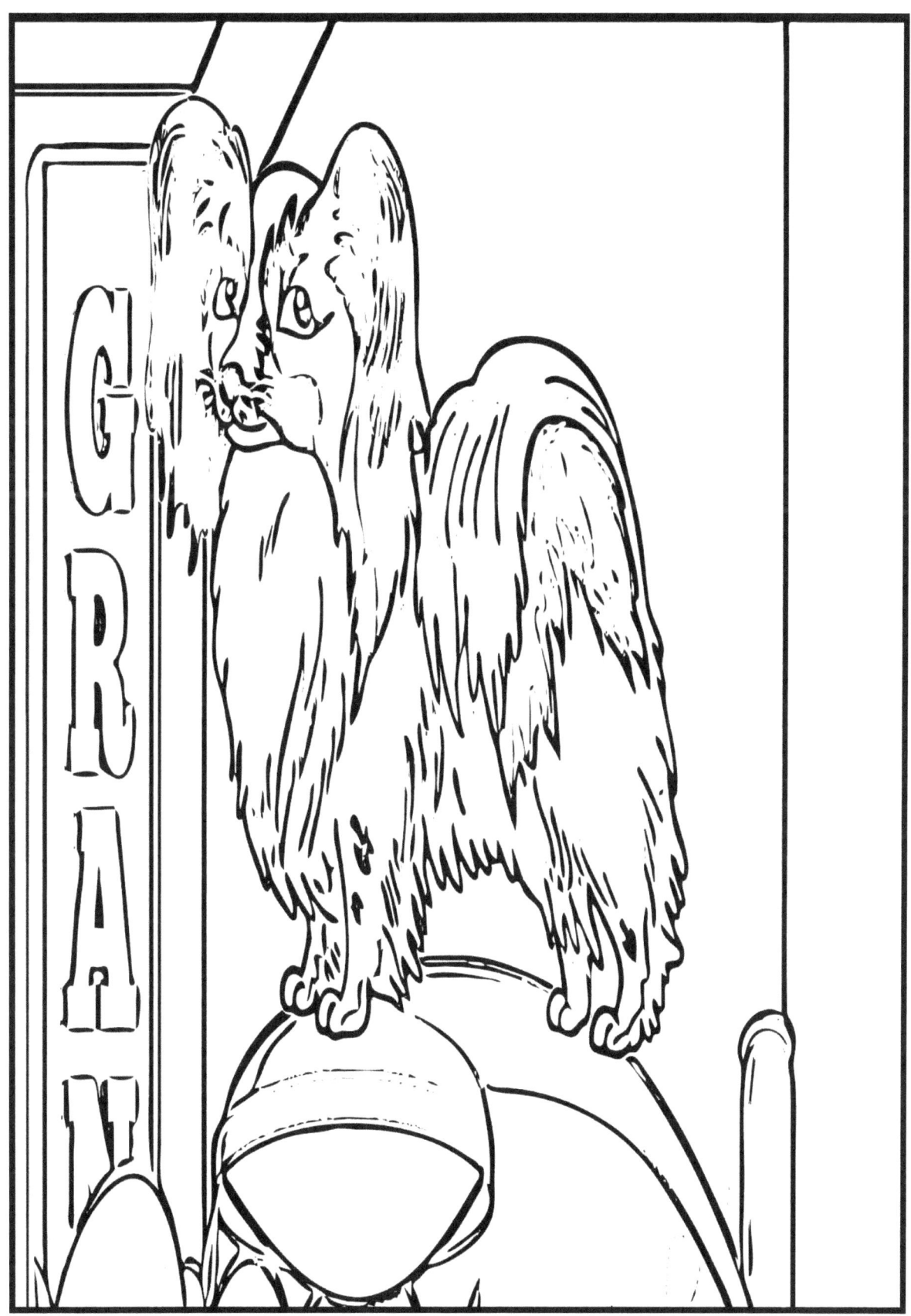

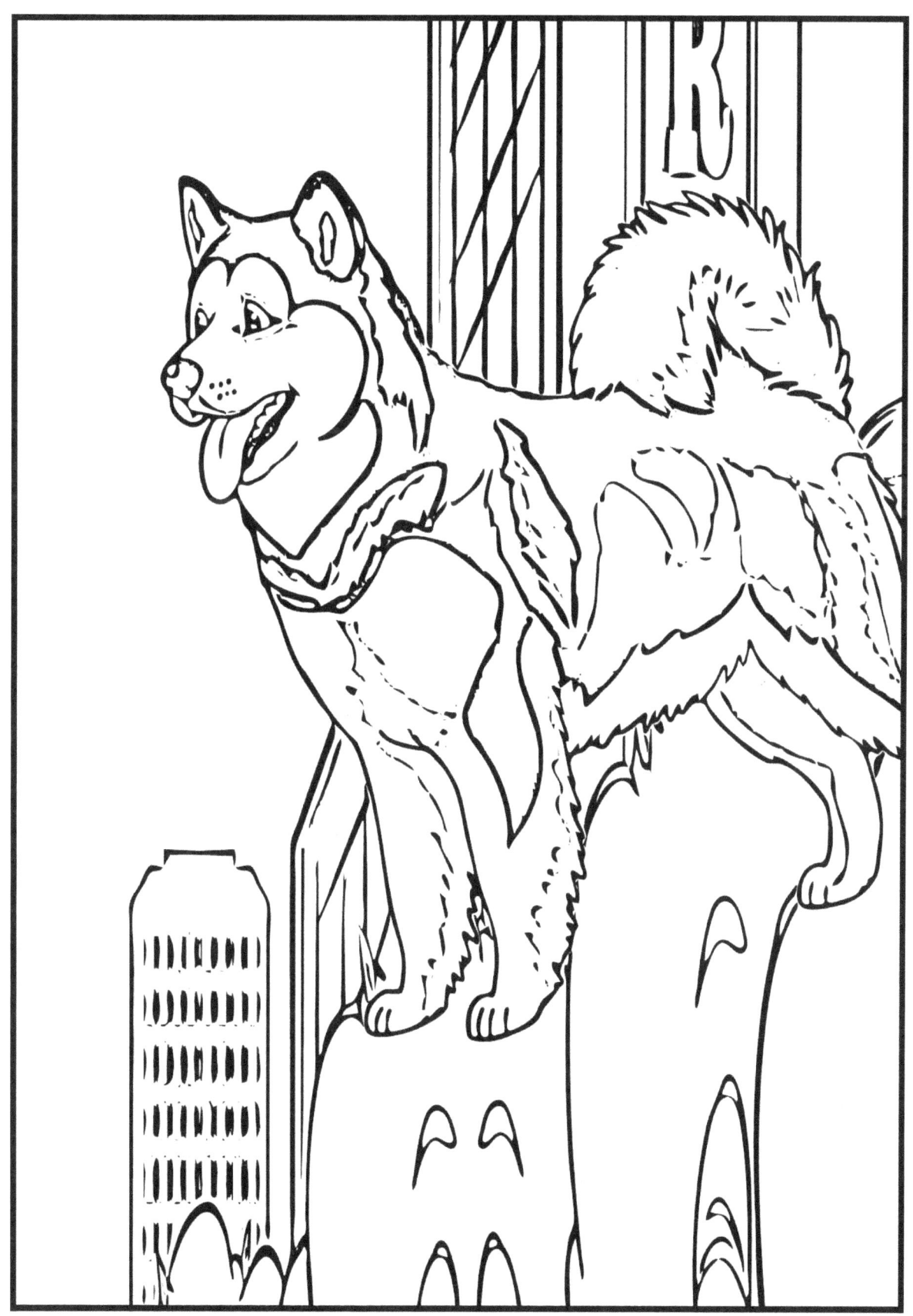

www.ingramcontent.com/pod-product-compliance
Lightning Source LLC
Chambersburg PA
CBHW080832180526
45168CB00006B/2648